Stephen Poliakoff

D0140984

BREAKING
THE SILENCE

METHUEN · LONDON AND NEW YORK

A METHUEN PAPERBACK

First published in Great Britain in 1984 as a Methuen New
Theatrescript by Methuen London Ltd, 11 New Fetter Lane,
London EC4P 4EE and in the United States of America in 1985
by Methuen Inc, 29 West 35th Street, New York, NY 10001

This second, completely revised and reset, post-production
edition published in the Methuen Modern Plays series in 1986 by
Methuen London Ltd and Methuen Inc.

Printed in Great Britain by
Richard Clay (The Chaucer Press) Ltd,
Bungay, Suffolk

Author's Note

This play was suggested by what happened to my family in Russia after the Bolshevick Revolution. But it is a work of fiction. I reworked and reshaped events, and invented the relationships and all the characters, *inspired* by the true image of my grandfather, a figure immaculately dressed for the opera, who did for a time have his own train, chugging through Lenin's Russia.

A man of great inventive brilliance, to whose memory I dedicate this play.

Breaking the Silence was first presented by the Royal Shakespeare Company at the Pit in the Barbican Centre, London on 31 October 1984 with the following cast:

NIKOLAI	Daniel Massey
EUGENIA	Gemma Jones
POLYA	Juliet Stevenson
VERKOFF	John Kane
SASHA	Jason Lake
GUARD 1	Richard Garnett
GUARD 2	Campbell Morrison

Directed by Ron Daniels
Designed by Alison Chitty

It transferred to the Mermaid Theatre, London, on 16 May 1985 with the following cast:

NIKOLAI	Alan Howard
EUGENIA	Gemma Jones
POLYA	Jenny Agutter
VERKOFF	John Kane
SASHA	Edward Rawle-Hicks
GUARD 1	Paul Rattee
GUARD 2	Christopher Saul

Directed by Ron Daniels
Designed by Alison Chitty

Time: Russia, 1920

ACT ONE

April, 1920

Scene One

Sound of people struggling with the door, then it opens, throwing a little light inside, and POLYA *and* SASHA *move into the darkened carriage.*

The huge imperial-style railway carriage, filling the whole of the stage.

Rich dark wood, a table, chairs set against the walls, at one end a splendid couch elaborately decorated, which had been converted into a bed, at the other end two bunks covered in pale velvet counterpanes, a white stove built into the wall, ornamental woodwork and lamps.

Over the beds and on parts of the floor, there is a coating of dirt, dust, a few bloodstains, some animal droppings, smudging the atmosphere of magnificence in the carriage. The pale bed coverings are especially filthy. The blinds across the windows are also stained yellow and black.

POLYA *is in her early thirties dressed in a black maid's dress, with a white bow in her hair.* SASHA *at the start of the action is in his early teens, but looks young for his age, immaculately dressed in a velvet suit.*

For a second POLYA *stands in the doorway staring into the darkened carriage then she moves in, pulling up the blinds, to let in light. As she enters the carriage she is carrying two highly polished pigskin suitcases.* SASHA *is only carrying some rather grubby toy stuffed animal.*

POLYA. Stay there Master Alexander (*as she moves into the darkened carriage alone:*) and don't touch, you understand, don't touch anything.

She pulls up the blinds to reveal the state of the carriage.

They certainly haven't bothered to clean it for your father.

SASHA (*in doorway*). What an extraordinary carriage, Polya . . . What was it used for?

POLYA. Don't come in! I told you, stay there by the door until I know it's safe for you . . . there might be something here that can harm you. Something that could give you a disease.

She moves away from the windows into the carriage, as an advance guard.

Whatever this smell is . . . I don't think the original passengers would have smelled like that.

SASHA (*pointing at floor*). What are those?

POLYA. Animal droppings — they must have used it for transporting livestock recently. That's why the beds have been chewed.

SASHA (*moving a little deeper into the carriage*). They can't really mean this Polya! . . . It needs hosing down before it's nearly ready for papa. You must have misunderstood. I am sure they only intend to show it to him . . .

POLYA (*loud, swings round*). Did I say it was safe for you to come in? No.

SASHA *stops.*

You can stay there now, but don't move. (*She turns back to her beds.*) Now don't you start causing me trouble, they haven't allowed me any time to make it fit for the master. (*She is rolling up the counterpanes.*) The filth that is here . . . he will never sleep in sheets like this, not under any circumstances, nobody could make him. I don't know how I am going to keep my uniform clean.

With the removal of the stained counterpanes, the carriage is already looking less filthy.

SASHA (*as POLYA bustles around*). Everything is such a hurry now — suddenly the news that Papa has to leave home, having to pack his things up in a few hours, I am sure we dropped something on the way here . . . Papa will demand compensation I expect.

POLYA. If I can get these out of the way before they come, there must be at least one clean place for the master — thank God I managed to bring some extra blankets for him.

SASHA. What are these holes? (*He is running his hand along the side of the carriage.*) Polya everywhere here is covered in small holes.

POLYA. What do you think they are! Bullet holes of course. (*She points above the windows.*) There's some marks up there too . . . it looks as if it was shelled.

SASHA. They must be going to redecorate it. (*Exploring the carriage.*) What are these red stains here Polya? It's splashed all over here, over the covers here, it can't be what I think it is Polya. (*Pause.*) It's not blood is it?

POLYA. Yes, it's blood. The goats they kept, they probably slaughtered them in here as well.

She looks up to see SASHA *is suddenly very animated, searching all the corners of the carriage.*

What on earth are you doing? I told you not to touch anything.

SASHA. I was just seeing if there was any . . . (*He stops and faces her*:) even the smallest piece of . . . (*Suddenly shouts*:) *food* had been left anywhere. There's an onion here!

SASHA *picks up a glass jar with one onion at the bottom, he tries to unscrew the top which is very stiff. He can't get it off.*

I'm so — I'm so hungry Polya.

Suddenly letting his body go limp and falling into her arms.

I'm going to *die*.

POLYA. Your father has the rations, you know that. Stand up. (*Pulling her body up.*) Come on stand up. (*Firmly*:) Listen now Alexander Nikolaivitch, don't you *dare* show it when they come — you're not going to let the Commissar of Labour see the slightest sign, you understand. You don't want to let

your father down. (*Holding him.*) Come on. You can
manage . . . you can get through.

SASHA. I am going to die before the end of the day, I can feel it.

POLYA. Well wait till then at least − (*Turning back to the bed.*)
the master will see to everything, *remember* that.

EUGENIA *enters. A fine looking woman about forty. She has
a nervous, shy manner. She is dressed in an exquisite and
expensive long summer dress.*

EUGENIA. I didn't imagine it would look like this. (*Looking
around.*) This is rather sordid isn't it? These beds . . . (*She
touches them.*) What a place!

POLYA. Madame, careful where you move. If you want to sit, I
think this space is safe.

EUGENIA (*anxious*). I am not sure the master is expecting
this . . . have you got all his clothes prepared?

She gets up immediately and moves over.

Is this all there is left? All that remains of his wardrobe. It
looks so little suddenly. We had to leave so much . . .

POLYA. We still got all his English shoes.

She pulls them out of a suitcase.

EUGENIA. As far as possible everything must go in its proper
place. (*She turns suddenly.*) Do we look all right Polya, not
too pale, tell me honestly − we don't seem disgracefully pale
do we?

POLYA. No, madame.

EUGENIA (*trying to force the jar open*). It doesn't look as if I'm
about to collapse at any moment I hope.

POLYA (*indicating the jar*). It won't open, madame.

EUGENIA (*embarrassed, putting jar down*). I never used to eat
onions anyway.

SASHA *is holding his stomach, leaning against the wall of the
carriage.*

Sasha! Don't do that.

VERKOFF *comes into the carriage, a powerful burly man in utilitarian clothes, a man in his forties, with a working-class accent. He is full of a sudden, unpredictable energy. Mercurial manner.*

VERKOFF. We are here! (*He turns and looks behind him.*) Where is he? He was right behind me. What are you doing out there Nikolai Semenovitch? (*Loud.*) Get in here! My time is limited.

NIKOLAI *is in the doorway.*

What on earth are you looking so reluctant for? Come on in. Take the plunge.

NIKOLAI *is framed in the doorway. He is an imposing figure in his late forties or early fifties, wearing a truly splendid fur coat, though it is spring, gleaming polished shoes, and a fine English suit. His manner is extremely authoritative and dignified, though there is a very distinctive charm and lightness of touch even when he's being arrogant. Everything about him is redolent of an old world, upper middle-class man. The only thing he is carrying is a medium-sized mahogany box.*

NIKOLAI (*staring into the carriage*). My God . . .

VERKOFF (*moving round, touching everything*). What's the matter — you should feel at home here! Gold-topped taps — what looks like a German commode, right size for one anyway — imperial furniture.

VERKOFF *pulling at the bunks, suddenly jumps onto the lower bunk, scattering dried feathers.*

A little dirty perhaps, but you could sleep through anything in this (*Sharp smile.*) and you may *need* to.

NIKOLAI (*moving into the carriage, calmly*). Is there anywhere in this carriage that it is possible to sit?

EUGENIA (*nervously*). Here . . .

As NIKOLAI *sits next to* EUGENIA, VERKOFF *has resumed roaming the carriage.*

VERKOFF (*suddenly pointing at* SASHA). The boy looks terrified, you'll have to teach him not to look at people like that. (*He smiles.*) They could feel unappreciated.

NIKOLAI. He is just a little surprised like all of us.

VERKOFF. So I can see! (*He turns.*) You do understand Nikolai Semenovitch what is happening to you — (*Stopping and staring at him.*) You are now a government employee with all the responsibility that entails. You will take up the position — as of now (*Clicking his fingers.*) of Telephone Surveyor of the Northern Railway.

NIKOLAI (*looking up*). Telephone Surveyor?

VERKOFF. Yes, Surveyor. (*Pulling at pieces of the carriage, touching everything.*) You don't like it? He doesn't like that title, then we can change it . . . (*Sharp smile.*) The only thing that can be changed Nikolai Pesiakoff. Telephone Examiner is acceptable . . . you have just become the first Telephone Examiner of the Northern District.

Silence.

NIKOLAI. I thank you for this unexpected offer, for making the journey specially.

VERKOFF. Which I haven't . . .

NIKOLAI. But of course it is completely out of the question, I will have to refuse.

Pause.

VERKOFF (*loud*). You will have to refuse!

NIKOLAI (*calmly*). I am much too busy I'm afraid.

VERKOFF. Too busy, I don't believe this! You have just been sitting here in the country . . . this is not an *offer* Nikolai Semenovitch, there is no refusal possible. You are MADE Telephone Examiner, it has been decided, once you've been selected and put on board, there is no alternative, no argument — the matter is completely closed.

NIKOLAI (*calmly*). I see. (*Pause.*) I will still have to refuse.

VERKOFF. I don't think we understand each other, Nikolai Semenovitch, I am a busy man and have very little time.

NIKOLAI (*incisive tones*). But I have told you what I need. I made repeated representations to you and your staff, and was made to wait on more than one occasion, sitting on the floor outside your door. I travelled no fewer than six times to your office, I made it absolutely clear what I had to have.

VERKOFF (*slight smile*). Remind me what this was.

NIKOLAI. It was a very modest request, the bare minimum in fact. A room of my own in Moscow, apart from living quarters for my family of course, for the sake of argument say five rooms, a proper staff of my own prepared to work, and sufficient time free of interruption and official interference — to think.

VERKOFF (*incredulous*). To think!

NIKOLAI. Of course. I have some specific ideas of the greatest importance, I thought I gave your advisers all the indications they needed. And I have to admit I fail to see what the problem is, you have my word for it that you will not be wasting your time. What more do you need?

VERKOFF. Nikolai Semonovitch . . .

NIKOLAI (*carrying straight on*). Furthermore, you gave us absolutely no warning that this was about to happen, you suddenly inform us that you will be taking over our whole house.

VERKOFF (*ebullient*). Warning! You don't get any warning, you know about it when it happens to you.

NIKOLAI (*amazed tones*). And why me? How was I chosen? I'm afraid I am not the right person to watch telephone poles being erected.

EUGENIA (*nervous*). My husband means that he . . .

NIKOLAI (*calmly*). In the chaos of a new filing system it is obvious there must have been a mistake, stumbling on me to be Telephone Surveyor is not a rational act, do I look a likely candidate? It is not a disgrace to admit there has been an error and have it rectified — immediately.

VERKOFF (*mercurial smile*). There is no possibility of an error I assure, *I* made the decision personally — you were after all supposedly head of your family's engineering firm were you not? How many times you were ever there is another question of course.

NIKOLAI. We did not concern ourselves with telephone poles.

VERKOFF. Don't try to test my patience — it can have dramatic results.

He points at the women and SASHA.

You three will pack up *all* your belongings (*Slight smile.*) in that sizeable house of yours, which I'm told the Army needs, and be ready to move immediately he returns.

EUGENIA (*very nervous*). Move where, comrade?

VERKOFF. You will all live in here, of course.

NIKOLAI (*momentary pause*). That is clearly impossible. In no circumstances can I allow my wife to live inside here.

VERKOFF (*loud, very animated*). Listen to him! My God, there have been people dying all along the line, whole households starving, wiped out, and he complains about being here.

VERKOFF'*s bulky shape moving about the carriage, his hand jabbing out.*

I have many urgent calls to make before the light goes . . . Now, this is where thing get serious. There are certain things you have to know and do, so you better be listening. (*He suddenly swings round and shouts.*) Are you comrade?

NIKOLAI *looks up in surprise.*

Because these matter.

NIKOLAI *is impassive.*

EUGENIA. Of course . . . we do realise . . .

VERKOFF (*staring at them*). *Guns.* (*He pauses.*) There must be no guns of any sort kept here. You are civilians — as you know, new laws have been passed — any civilian found with firearms or explosives will be executed. (*Sudden sharp smile.*) If you have any, this is not a time to be shy, give them to me and no action will be taken.

NIKOLAI. That is the law? I had no idea.

VERKOFF. Are you going to give them to me? I urge you to take this seriously comrade, otherwise the consequences for you and your family could be disastrous.

Silence.

NIKOLAI. Quite. Thank you for your warning. There is no need to labour the point. What is next?

VERKOFF. You are required to keep ledgers, official records that must be up to date. The exact times and places, and the progress you find. I am giving you ten thousand roubles.

He throws the money, which is in a bag, on the floor of the carriage at NIKOLAI's *feet.*

This will be used for railway business only, the bonus scheme we have in operation for rewarding good work, all the usual things.

NIKOLAI. What is usual for a Telephone Examiner?

VERKOFF. You will take this first trip, which will be a gruelling one, and then you will wait in a siding for further instructions.

NIKOLAI. In a *siding*? That can't be necessary . . .

VERKOFF (*ignoring this*). If you ever wish to summon a locomotive in an emergency, you will walk the eighteen miles down the line and use the railway telephone to the depot. (*He points suddenly at* EUGENIA.) What's your name?

EUGENIA (*nervously glancing about her*). My name . . . you mean me? It's Eugenia Michailovna.

VERKOFF (*staring straight at her*). You think he's been listening, Eugenia Michailovna? You ought to make him. People have been turned off trains before now, in the North, and made to walk the thousand miles home. (*Lightly.*) I wonder how he'd manage.

NIKOLAI *is sitting impassively in his fur coat.* VERKOFF

suddenly turns towards POLYA.

And *you*, what's your name? What is your position here?

POLYA. I am the second chamber maid, comrade — I mean I *was* in Moscow, there was me and Anya . . . (*Suddenly nervous.*) and Liuba who cooked. (*She looks away, embarrassed.*) I . . . I was going to be married to the porter of an apartment block near us in Moscow but we lost touch . . . with all the moving round the country. (*She stops.*) I'm sorry, my name's Polya.

VERKOFF. And you're going to *stay* with this lot?

POLYA. Yes comrade, I have nowhere else to go. (*Looking down at the floor.*) At the moment anyway.

VERKOFF (*moves swiftly across the carriage to* NIKOLAI). Your pass and badge of office. Wear that at all times.

NIKOLAI (*as it is pinned on his fur coat*). My dear fellow, I assure you this is a major blunder, I urge you to reconsider while there's still time.

VERKOFF (*turning at the door of the carriage*). I almost forgot the most important thing — what about food?

SASHA (*from the heart*). Food!

VERKOFF (*mercurial smile at* SASHA). Yes, do you remember what it was like. (*To the adults*:) Have you got enough, do you need some?

Agonised look from SASHA, EUGENIA *looks at* NIKOLAI *and then away. They wait for* NIKOLAI. *Silence.*

NIKOLAI. No that will not be necessary.

VERKOFF. You're sure? You wouldn't be stupid enough to be too proud to ask — I'd have no patience with that.

He watches their faces as he mentions each piece of food.

I can supply some eggs, meat, fresh cheese, smoked fish, fresh bread. (*He smiles.*) That would mean soft doughy bread, baked today, like these rolls.

He produces large rolls out of his deep pockets. EUGENIA *and* SASHA *turn away trying not to look at them.* VERKOFF *holds out the bread.*

Everybody looks away do they?

SASHA (*desperately*). Maybe we . . .

VERKOFF (*sharp moving*). So you have managed to farm all your own food, unlike nearly everybody else in this area. I'm delighted to hear it.

He leaves the bread lying conspicuously. Pointing at EUGENIA.

You look magnificent madame. (*He stops in the doorway.*) You are now working for me Nikolai Semenovitch — the Northern Railway and me. I don't know when we'll be seeing each other again but we certainly will be — (*With feeling:*) I hope you're not going to let me down.

VERKOFF *exits. As soon as he's gone,* SASHA *bolts over and gets the bread he left behind.* EUGENIA *also makes a move, less violent but almost as eager.*

NIKOLAI. Don't disgrace yourself Sasha — charging after food like a starving dog.

EUGENIA (*taking the bread*). Shall I? I'll divide it up.

NIKOLAI (*waving his portion away*). We do not need food from him. We are certainly not going to accept food like beggars.

The women and SASHA *are feasting on the bread.*

I will leave you with all the rations we have, including my own. And I will bring food home. I will provide all the food we need and more.

SASHA *licks every crumb that is left.*

POLYA. Make it last . . . not so quick Sasha, make it last as long as you can.

EUGENIA (*smiling*). One's body can't cope with the shock at all. (*She leans against the wall.*)

NIKOLAI (*calmly*). It appears we have been selected to spend time in these surroundings — something I didn't anticipate. So on my return we will divide it up. Eugenia . . . this will be your room. (*He indicates the area in the middle of the carriage.*) The child will be over there. (*Pointing to the bunks.*) Polya's quarters will be down there, (*Pointing to the area near the bunks.*) and the rest will be for my use, study, bedroom and morning room combined. (*He indicates the rest of the carriage.*) We will keep to these. We may be able to arrange partitions when I return . . .

The noise of a locomotive approaching in the distance — calling down the line.

POLYA (*frantic*). His clothes and bed are not ready. I haven't had a chance to make it even passable for you Barin. You will be away so long, and there hasn't nearly been time to unpack.

Both women flit about the carriage like terrified bats, with the sound of the locomotive getting louder.

POLYA (*laying out his clothes*). The only pair of pyjamas that are left . . .

NIKOLAI. There is no need to panic, they will wait for us.

EUGENIA (*stopping, staring at him*). Nikolai, I think . . . please don't be angry with me . . . I think you will need me to come with you. Who will put out your clothes, with no manservant, and Liuba gone as well, nobody to do your laundry, find things for you to wear each day?

POLYA. It's not a job for you, Madame.

EUGENIA. Let me come Nikolai, I won't be in the way, I won't touch anything. You know I won't bother you. You will never notice me, but you *need* someone . . . can I come? Please, (*Suddenly loud.*) please let me come. I can make it all easier for you. (*Loud.*) Let me . . .

NIKOLAI. That will not be possible my dear.

POLYA. You can't go on your own, Barin, I must come . . .

EUGENIA. Make him see sense.

NIKOLAI. Polya you must stay with Madame. She must have the very best that is possible in the circumstances. (*To* EUGENIA:) Do nothing without Polya's help my dear.

The locomotive really loud and close, the sound of it braking and coming to a halt.

I will take the boy — if he thinks he can manage the journey,
I will take Sasha.

SASHA (*excited*). Me Papa? You want to take me?

The sound of the locomotive hissing to a halt.

EUGENIA. Is that sensible Nikolai? Neither of you are used to
being on your own, he can't organise everything for you, Sasha
can't deal with everything.

SASHA. I can, I will.

NIKOLAI. I am going to take the boy.

EUGENIA (*urgent*). We must get more clothes for him, he'll need
them for the cold.

POLYA (*urgent*). It'll take at least two hours to get to the house
and back, and I don't know how much is washed, how much is
clean.

EUGENIA (*moving*). Quickly, Polya, we'll have to go and get
them.

EUGENIA *looking back.* POLYA *goes.*

NIKOLAI. Don't worry, we will not leave before you come back.

EUGENIA (*in doorway*). You won't . . . you won't take any risks
Kolia, you know it could be dangerous, please try to be more
careful than usual.

NIKOLAI. Don't worry. They will know who I am.

EUGENIA *goes. Silence.*
NIKOLAI *staring across at* SASHA.

We will be alone together you and I.

SASHA. Yes, Papa.

NIKOLAI. Certain things have to be understood — the terms on
which we accompany each other. (*He pauses.*) Sashenka, can
you pass me that box, yes that one there, give it to me.

SASHA *gives him the mahogany box he came in with.*

I have something vital to occupy me — something of the
highest importance. If certain actions are taken — by me — it

will be because of that. At the moment nothing more can be discussed.

He takes a pistol out of the mahogany box, it gleams in the light.

Do you understand me?

SASHA. Yes, Papa.

NIKOLAI (*with gun*). There will be no problem, nobody will dare touch us.

Blackout.

Scene Two

The noise of the train immediately filling the blackout, moving through the night, changing into the wail of the locomotive, then into screaming brakes, the sound of their progress violently stuttering to a halt, then silence.

The night carriage. The blinds are down. The lights glowing. SASHA's arms are wrapped around himself; he is now wearing a miniature version of his father's magnificent coat, and he is pulling it tightly round him. NIKOLAI is sitting bolt upright and still.

SASHA. Papa — we've stopped. (*Moving to the window.*) I think we've arrived somewhere again.

NIKOLAI. We will not have heard of it whatever it's called.

Pause.

SASHA. It's very cold anyway! God my hands, I can hardly move them. (*Moving away from the window.*) I'm going to eat my rations for today, Papa.

NIKOLAI. It is up to you when you eat.

NIKOLAI *remains absolutely still. Silence.*

SASHA (*picking up a small brown morsel*). Except the taste of dried millet is beginning to be . . . rather revolting . . .

NIKOLAI. I have told you — use your imagination. What is it

there for? Transform the food.

SASHA. Will you do it for me again?

SASHA *begins to eat as* NIKOLAI *proceeds.*

NIKOLAI. Imagine the delicate flesh, fish . . . fresh baked with a touch of sorrel the way Liuba used to cook it for us, pink, with a little butter, and flaking . . . (*Suddenly stopping, sharp.*) How long is it since we left in this — how many days now?

SASHA. I am not sure, we have stood still so often with just blackness out there, they don't even have stars here! I've got lost, I think.

NIKOLAI (*calmly*). You promised me you were keeping count Sasha — what month is it, we must know that, is it still May?

SASHA. I think it's May, or June, May . . .

NIKOLAI. Put it up on the wall, say it is now Day 21, notch it up on the wall. We start serious counting from now on, you must not lose count again, time has become important.

Sudden violent knocking on the door.

Make yourself respectable.

SASHA *is pushing his hair straight, and at the same time picking crumbs of food off his coat.*

SASHA. Is there anything here people shouldn't find papa, that we should move before . . .

The door crashes open and two pale faced GUARDS *in military uniform burst into the carriage with startling ferocity.* GUARD 1 *is tall, thin, and in his late twenties,* GUARD 2 *is burly, about ten years older, unshaven, hands stained with nicotine. Both* GUARDS *are armed.*

GUARD 1. Right!

He stops for a second in surprise at seeing NIKOLAI *resplendent in his coat, sitting on the magnificence of the carriage.*

All right — could you stand up please. (*Sharp.*) Come on stand up.

GUARD 2 (*fast*). State your destination — arrival date, departure date, and nature of your business.

GUARD 1. We need to see your travel permit and your identification card, where are they?

GUARD 2. We're going to look at your luggage as well, so lay it out along here . . .

NIKOLAI. My dear comrades, none of that need concern us.

NIKOLAI *has remained seated,* SASHA *has stood.*

GUARD 1. What do you mean that doesn't concern us — everything that comes down this line concerns us.

GUARD 2. Where are you going for a start?

NIKOLAI (*simply*). I have no idea.

GUARD 1. Do you know where you are now?

NIKOLAI. I have even less idea of that — a remote settlement where it seems people have the sense not to live. (*He smiles.*) I assume you didn't choose to be here. (*He looks straight at both of them.*) Gentlemen, through some appalling error — for which I have yet to find the culprit — I am your new Telephone Examiner.

Silence.

GUARD 1 (*momentarily astonished*). You mean you . . . you work for the Northern Railway?

NIKOLAI. For the moment, yes. Why else do you think I would be here? (*He points to* SASHA.) That over there is my son who is accompanying me on this mission. (*Smiles.*) We are not going to waste our time in not believing each other, I would hardly invent such a story — there is no obvious advantage for me in having to wander up and down the line . . . unless I officially *had* to.

Slight pause.

GUARD 1. No, we believe you.

GUARD 2 (*smiles*). If you say that's who you are — we believe you.

GUARD 1. Forgive us comrade, we have been here so long, and we haven't seen anyone for several months, not since the men working on the line left.

GUARD 2 (*sharp smile*). All we see is the occasional freight train, we wait by the line praying for lights to appear, howling for a train! And when one comes all we get are people staring down from the locomotive as they rumble past . . .

GUARD 1. But comrades we don't have much news here about telephones to give you — the poles haven't even arrived yet.

NIKOLAI (*calmly*). I expected as much.

GUARD 2. Where are you from comrade — which depot are you from?

NIKOLAI. I'm afraid I have never been inside a depot. We are from Moscow, though we have been in the country for . . .

GUARD 2 (*cutting him off*). Moscow! — you're from Moscow. (*To* GUARD 1:) He's from *Moscow*, at last we've got someone.

Both GUARDS *exploding with excitement, questions tumbling out, cutting each other's sentences.*

GUARD 1 (*loud*). How are things there?

GUARD 2. There's so much you'll have to tell us . . .

GUARD 1. What is happening? What is the latest news, are things easier, are more goods getting through to the shops?

GUARD 2. Will we recognise the place? Are all the streets renamed? Is the new station built? They were just starting it, it was going to be enormous!

GUARD 1. Is there still fighting in the East — are things quieter now?

GUARD 2 (*earthy smile*). What sort of moving pictures are playing in Moscow — have you any of the latest jokes, we need a few!

GUARD 1. We've had to sense what's been happening, imagine it all, from this distance.

GUARD 2. We've missed so much already! We caught somebody's eye at the wrong moment.

GUARD 1. We must have looked dumb enough!

GUARD 2. Tell us what the good news is, start with that and . . .

NIKOLAI (*cutting them off and holding up his hand*). Gentlemen. Quiet. (*Pause.*) I have no news I'm afraid.

GUARD 2. None? At all . . .

NIKOLAI. None. (*Facing them, calmly.*) But we can do a transaction. We have little time to do it . . . we have a drunken driver who decides to take off suddenly and with little warning . . . so listen carefully because this is a matter of the utmost urgency. (*He pauses for this to sink in.*) I need the following — which I am sure you will be able to provide. I need some foreign newspapers — any foreign newspaper. Any scrap of especially English or American journals you have, any stray piece that may have come into your possession off the trains from the northern ports.

GUARD 2 (*taking it in*). Foreign newspapers . . . foreign news.

NIKOLAI. Second, I need some metal goods, any spare objects made out of metal of a transportable size, any metal appliances generally, everything you have.

GUARD 2. Metal appliances?

NIKOLAI (*suddenly to* SASHA). Have I left anything out? (*Sharper.*) Come on, have I?

SASHA. Me, Papa?! . . . *No.*

NIKOLAI (*calm smile*). I am willing to pay for this of course, that goes without saying — I will pay one thousand roubles if what you supply is satisfactory.

GUARD 1 (*bewildered*). One thousand roubles! As I understand it — all you want is some rubbish.

GUARD 2 (*grins*). We only have a limited amount of that round here — it's a very small station, take one step through the door and you've seen all there is to see.

GUARD 1. We get a few odd things off passing trains, and there's some of the debris from the two large estates that were about fifty miles from here and were burnt by bandits, we've got a little of that.

GUARD 2. It's all charred that stuff, you know it's burnt — (*Grins, eager to help.*) You want some of that comrade? We can arrange it . . .

NIKOLAI (*suddenly standing up*). I think I will have to examine it for myself. (*To* GUARD 2:) Show me the way.

NIKOLAI *exits with* GUARD 2.

SASHA (*loud*). Papa!

SASHA *is alone with the tall* GUARD.

GUARD 1 (*looking at* SASHA). This is a magnificent carriage, comrade.

SASHA. It needs cleaning.

The GUARD *is moving around the carriage fascinated, looking at everything.*

You should have seen our apartment in Moscow, we had nine or ten rooms like this, with grand pianos in three of them . . . my father has very high standards, he has the best of everything, usually.

GUARD 1 (*discovering with relish books in the carriage*). Books! Quite new! — I've had to read the same three books here over and over again. (*Flicking the pages of the official book, intrigued smile.*) There is nothing in the ledger — none of the stops you have made have been recorded.

SASHA (*thinking quickly*). That was deliberate on my father's part — if we'd been captured by bandits there would have been no record.

GUARD 1 (*looking at* NIKOLAI's *clothes*). That is an extraordinary coat your father is wearing. (*Friendly smile.*) He's a very exotic visitor for us, something special. (*Turning to* SASHA's *coat.*) All these clothes are foreign aren't they? (*Holding* SASHA's *coat.*) The smell of women, I can detect that even after weeks; English clothes are they?

GUARD 1 *moves on, looking near the box with the gun in it.*

SASHA (*watching closely*). My father likes English things — even the pigs on our estate had English names, before they all died

— Victoria, Hubert, Neville, and Lancelot, and Westminster.

GUARD 1 (*picking up the box of guns*). What are these?

SASHA (*before the* GUARD *can open it*). I think you may be exceeding your authority, my father said none of this must be touched. It's all *Railway* business.

GUARD 1. I just want a look, I won't do any harm.

SASHA (*really sharp*). Do you know who my father is — he's one of the most important men in Russia.

GUARD 1 (*taken aback*). He is?

SASHA (*loud*). Yes, you're not being visited by any old Telephone Examiner — by a run-of-the-mill official just dropping in out of the night, he's one of the most significant people you're ever likely to meet.

GUARD 1. Why?

SASHA. Why? What do you mean why? (*Suddenly unable to answer.*) Because . . . he is a man of importance.

NIKOLAI *enters, followed by* GUARD 2, *wheeling a baby carriage, an ornate low baby carriage with faded roses painted on the side and full of charred remains from the great estate.*

GUARD 2 (*smiling at* SASHA *who is staring in surprise*). You won't be able to fit in this easily will you!

NIKOLAI (*indicating a corner*). Leave it there . . . Sasha, pass me the money.

SASHA *carries across the bag of money.*

Gentlemen, looking at this — (NIKOLAI *indicates the baby carriage.*) it is clear we will have to do better. (*Holding out the money.*) I am going to give you the one thousand roubles, some of which is for this, some of which is in advance for what you are still going to find for me — before we leave.

GUARD 1. You want some more?

NIKOLAI. And in return, if I have the opportunity — I will use my new office to put in a word for you. Gentlemen, I will recommend you be moved to a better and more important posting. Include your personal details in the next consignment you bring for me.

GUARD 2 (*really loud*). We'll be back! (*Rushing to the door.*) Don't you go till we're back. We'll certainly be back with more.

Both GUARD 1 *and* 2 *exit with urgency.*

NIKOLAI (*indicating the baby carriage immediately.*) Are there any newspapers in there — have a look.

As SASHA *searches through the charred remains.*

We travel over a thousand miles — to find two young men going insane with loneliness! Feeling they're missing everything. The taller one is a pleasant boy, reminded me of one of the servants who left us for the war. Where are they now? I can't even remember what some of them looked like. The one with the rolling walk, what was his name? (*Suddenly back to* SASHA:) Have you found some Sasha? Bring me what you've got . . .

SASHA *is moving over, handing him fragments.*

I've had no foreign news for so long — and this is the best they could do, like bringing water to a man dying of thirst but only a few drops at a time . . . (*Staring at tattered pieces of newspaper.*) Where is this form? England, that's good . . . that's very good.

SASHA *also has a piece.*

Look through your piece Sasha and tell me what you find.

SASHA. What am I looking for Papa?

NIKOLAI. This does not look like a useful part of the paper — garden parties and the obituary page. Dead diplomats. Find the date — it is vital we find the date. (*Without a pause.*) Have you found it?

SASHA. It's in English, Papa!

NIKOLAI. All that education he was given, how many governesses were there — I lost count — and he can't even read the date in English.

SASHA (*struggling*). November 12, 1919.

NIKOLAI. My God! That's seven months ago. (*Incisive.*) That's the nearest we can get, and we don't even know *that,* because we've lost the current date as well. We will have to go through all this, Sasha, column by column, inch by inch. (*Tossing news scraps away.*) This paper smells of cats. We will have to continue this by daylight. Pass me that box, where's it gone? You know the one I mean, the one with the weapons inside it.

SASHA *is gingerly carrying the box for him.*

I just have to check to see if they are fully loaded.

SASHA. But you know they are. (*As the lid is raised:*) What are those other things in there?

NIKOLAI. Diamonds. Just a very few. All that is left — all that we were able to save from Moscow.

SASHA *moves to the stove, very nervous in case somebody comes in. The noise of the* GUARDS *as they search outside continues throughout the scene, with occasional banging against the back wall.*

SASHA. I will try to make the tea for you . . . I am getting better. I am still practising it.

He goes about it as if preparing for a major operation.

NIKOLAI (*glancing in* SASHA's *direction*). I will tell you an interesting fact — I have never felt a kettle. Certainly not when it has been boiling. I have never actually handled one. (*He smiles.*) I don't think I should start now.

SASHA (*looking at the guns*). They could come back at any moment Papa. (*Lowering his voice.*) Do you think they really turn people off trains like we were warned, making them walk into whatever's waiting for us out there.

NIKOLAI. It's more than possible. But why should anybody try to do that to us? Don't worry . . .

SASHA *turns back to the tea. Suddenly* NIKOLAI *lets out a really loud cry, an extraordinary and alarming wail of frustration.*

What the hell do I do?

SASHA *turns, truly startled.*

How do I manage it now? . . . prevent it escaping . . .

SASHA (*very worried*). What is it Papa? Are you unwell?

NIKOLAI (*voice dropping to a rapid murmur*). Being incarcerated alive . . . caged up like an animal . . . it's not possible now.

SASHA. What is it? What's the matter? (*Suddenly moving closer.*) What were you looking for in the paper? Tell me Papa.

NIKOLAI *is murmuring.*

What's happening? Tell me, please.

Silence.

NIKOLAI (*voice suddenly calm and authoritative again*). What have I always told you matters most, what is it our duty to do?

SASHA. To . . . to achieve, Papa?

NIKOLAI. Have you any idea what work I do?

Slight pause.

SASHA. No.

NIKOLAI. When I went into that large office, what do you suppose I was thinking about?

SASHA. Business?

NIKOLAI. Business — don't show your ignorance child, you make us sound like merchants.

NIKOLAI *is clutching the catch on the gun,* SASHA *watching, tense.*

Since there appears to be no one here, other than ourselves, who could be listening? (*He looks straight at* SASHA.) Nobody has ever been told what you are about to hear.

SASHA. No, Papa.

NIKOLAI *moves in the half-darkened carriage.*

NIKOLAI. If you were to think your father had found a way of

making the moving pictures talk — of recording sound on film
and then so enlarging the volume so the picture talks . . . If
you were to think I had found a way of doing this . . . (*Slight
pause.*) Almost, nearly . . . you would be right.

SASHA (*very quiet*). You've done that! Nearly done that!

NIKOLAI. *Nearly,* yes. In Moscow, I'd found a way of printing
sound directly onto film, but I can't unlock the answer to the
final stage, how to *enlarge* the sound. The problem is
frustratingly simple and the equipment required is reasonably
rudimentary. If I can do that . . .

Noise of GUARDS *outside.*

Why do you look so alarmed? You're old enough not to be
terrified of ideas. If I succeed Sasha, of course I will be the
first person in the world to do it.

SASHA (*hushed*). The first one . . . of all?

NIKOLAI. Which will have a considerable effect on all our lives.
Not merely fame, recognition on an international scale, but it
will give me the power to acquire the resources and staff I
need.

SASHA. That was why you were looking in the paper.

NIKOLAI. Yes, to see if on their theatre pages there is a
comment on such and such a film performer's voice.

SASHA. Do you think they could have done it already? Before
you?

NIKOLAI. No. I am fairly certain I am three or four years ahead
of the rest of the world. Naturally I have no evidence for that,
such a proposition is by its very nature unprovable, until I, or
somebody else, achieves it. But I *sense* I am ahead. But we
must not dwell on that. If I think all the time about being
overtaken — we will go insane.

Silence.

SASHA. I have never been to the moving pictures.

NIKOLAI. Neither have I.

SASHA (*surprised*). *You* haven't Papa?

NIKOLAI. No, never. Not in public.

SASHA (*suddenly, seeing his father still holding the gun*). Papa, if they find you with your guns now, it may not help you.

NIKOLAI. They won't ever come in here without knocking.

Noise of GUARDS' *voices from outside.*

It is interesting, Sasha, don't you think, how time and time again the same idea happens in totally separate places at the same time — in completely different parts of the globe. They come out of the ether together. Simultaneous progress . . . But on this I have a real start.

SASHA. Yes, Papa . . .

NIKOLAI (*smiles. Suddenly really loud*). BUT, MY GOD, THE ODDS, SASHA — the odds against us are enormous. I am at least one thousand miles from Moscow, shut up in this wooden box — alone with a child. And on my return, the *women* have to live inside here, have to share this space with us . . . (*Pause.*) . . . a situation so bizarre I can hardly believe I have allowed it to happen to me.

SASHA. I will help, I can do things.

Noise of the GUARDS.

NIKOLAI. I didn't know such vastness, such space out there and being alone, could be so disturbing, left without our staff, servants, without any support.

SASHA (*very quiet*). It frightens me too, Papa.

NIKOLAI. You must never admit to being frightened, Sasha. (*Tone lightening, picking up the money*.) At least there is one unexpected advantage — I have been given plenty of money.

SASHA. For railway business . . . isn't it?

NIKOLAI (*suddenly looking at him sharply.*) Have you taken in what I have just said Sasha?

SASHA. Of course, Papa.

NIKOLAI. Look at me — look at me straight in the eye. You must learn to look people directly in the eye, anything else makes you seem dishonest.

SASHA. Yes.

NIKOLAI. It is stating the obvious Sasha — but this is a night of grave importance between us, more than any other.

SASHA. I know, Papa.

NIKOLAI (*firmly*). What are you afraid of now?

SASHA (*trying not to sound scared*). I am not anymore . . . I won't be.

NIKOLAI (*calmly*). Stand up and face me, and give me your word you will never repeat to anyone what you have heard tonight. (*Pause.*) The work must never be discussed in front of the women, or anyone, you understand.

Pause.

SASHA. I give you my word.

NIKOLAI. Good. (*Calmly touches his coat.*) You must be careful to keep up your appearance, Sashenka, especially when meeting ordinary soldiers like tonight . . .

They look at each other .

You may go back to your room now.

SASHA (*moving across the width of the carriage*). It is a kind of race isn't it, Papa, what we're in?

NIKOLAI. In a way.

SASHA. And you'll come first?

NIKOLAI. There can only be one result. (*Louder:*) Let neither of us be in any doubt what is at stake from this moment on. It will need such energy Sasha.

Suddenly lifting the gun — pointing at the ceiling.

My God what are we doing still here! If they are not coming back, we are being kept waiting for no useful purpose. (*Very loud:*) Come on you drunken bastard we've got to be underway now. Get this thing moving!

He lifts the gun, about to pull the trigger.

SASHA (*screaming*). Papa! Remember!

NIKOLAI (*turning*). Remember what! They won't dare to bother us. But maybe we don't want holes in the roof — not till we get back to the South.

The door is thrown open, light pouring in. NIKOLAI *makes no attempt to conceal the gun.* GUARD 1 *moves into the doorway of the carriage and throws a large black bag of extra junk inside. It clanks as it hits the floor.*

GUARD 1 (*friendly smile*). We found everything we could, comrade! Every scrap there is. You'll soon be off now. Our names and personal histories are in there too, comrade, don't lose them! *We will meet again.* (*Smiles.*) When the new phone exchange is opened, we'll make the first calls! Goodbye, comrade, we won't forget you.

NIKOLAI. Thank you my friend. I will not forget your promotion. If you get your release you'll be more fortunate than I.

As the door is closing.

And comrade, tell our driver he is not to stop, don't let us stop at all now, till we hit the sea!

Blackout.

Scene Three

A hot sticky late summer afternoon in the carriage, the two women, EUGENIA *and* POLYA, *are alone.*

    EUGENIA *is dressed in a full-length white dress, long sleeves, lavishly dressed as if to entertain friends for an evening meal, but her clothes are now stained and streaked with dirt from months of being in the carriage. She is sweating profusely, constantly wiping her face.* POLYA, *dressed in a black uniform but with bare legs, is kneeling on the carriage floor; between deep intakes of breath she is half singing, half talking down a speaking tube, the sort that could have come from a large house. It snakes out of the carriage door, which is just open enough to let it through. There is a partition around* NIKOLAI's *area.*

POLYA *continues to half sing, half gabble into the tube.*

POLYA (*loud*). Can you hear this . . .? (*Then very quiet.*) Is this loud enough? . . . Seventy-seven, seventy-eight, seventy-nine, seventy-ten . . . You see, after a day of this I can't even count any more . . . my brain is throbbing. (*Loud:*) Can you hear it throbbing? (*Leaning her head forward:*) Should be ear-splitting? Can you hear me at all!

EUGENIA. He will stop soon, I'm sure he must finish with you any moment, it's not physically possible to go on much longer.

POLYA (*into the tube*). That's true of me, is it true of him? Maybe the Master needs a drink . . . (*Into the tube:*) He is beginning to feel thirsty now . . . getting a little cramped in that hut . . . he's just thinking how welcome a cool, slow drink would be . . . (*She continues to sing the song she began with very hoarsely.*) I used to sing this while doing the stairs in Moscow, the Master likes it. I don't think I ever want to hear it again after today.

She continues breathing into the speaking apparatus a smattering of song, and a nursery rhyme; her neck is soaked in sweat.

EUGENIA. If only he'd let me help you, he's always found the idea of me working extremely unpleasant. (*Nervous smile.*) He told me once he found the thought repulsive. (*Lightly:*) and I seem to be forbidden more than ever before to touch any of his work, even to glance at it. (*Looking at* POLYA *kneeling on the floor.*) Sometimes, Polya, I have an intense desire to go through everything of his.

POLYA (*into the tube*). Can the Master hear any of this . . .?

EUGENIA (*gently*). And now when he's divided up the carriage like the dacha, pinning us to this side (*She smiles.*) he's tried to shrink the house. (*She turns.*) You know I've never slept in public before, till these past months, not with somebody in the room other than Nikolai.

POLYA (*looking up*). Yes you squeezed yourself to the wall that first night didn't you, Madame . . . trying to hide in the luggage rack. (*Back to the tube.*) Thirsty . . . getting thirsty!

EUGENIA. Our neighbours, and my friends, would never believe this, that I ended up in this carriage . . .

POLYA (*finishing a verse of the song*). I wonder what I am doing all this for? (*Slight smile.*) After a time it does cross your mind, after fifty days, you do begin to get just a little curious. (*Into the tube:*) What's the answer? Are you still there?

EUGENIA. At least you don't have to dress like I do — in this heat. (*Holding herself.*) Do you know what it feels like shut up in this?

POLYA (*looking up*). I would go mad, Madame, if I had to wear that all the time.

EUGENIA. There are good reasons for it. (*She moves.*) As you know the Master always wants me to have the best, the best of everything. He needs to live like that, regardless of where he is. I shouldn't be saying this to you, Polya, but maybe because of us being Jewish, we were among the first Jewish families to be allowed to live in the capital. The Master, of course, has never considered himself inferior to anyone . . . so he always looked more part of Moscow society even than the oldest families, aristocratic in everything he chooses . . . everything he does. So I *have* to wear all this, it's what he wants of me. (*Looking at* POLYA, *she stops.*) I really oughtn't to say such things to you.

POLYA (*looking straight at her*). I know, Eugenia Michailovna . . . it's all right. (*Loud into the tube:*) I am sure the Master is no longer there. (*Calling down:*) Are you? He's walked off and left me singing to an empty railway line. (*Loud.*) So he won't notice, if I quite . . . suddenly . . . just . . . (*Very loud.*) stop.

POLYA *gets up and moves away.*

EUGENIA. Is that wise, Polya?

POLYA. We'll see if there is any reaction.

She is by the window.

I can't see him anywhere.

EUGENIA. I wonder if I dare take these off? (*Self-mocking smile, indicating her stockings.*) Do you think I should take the risk? If he notices you know how violently angry he can get. (EUGENIA *hesitates.*)

POLYA. Go on, he's too busy to notice.

EUGENIA *is pulling off her shoes and stockings.*

EUGENIA. I suppose, Polya, this must seem foolish to you, a grown woman making such a business of taking her shoes and stockings off, making it seem an important event, but for me it is. (*Smile.*) Bare legs in the sun. (*She stretches her legs out.*) My God that feels so good! (*She fans her dress.*) Sweat trickling out, fresh air! Polya, why has it taken me this long? (*She moves to the window.*)

POLYA. See he *hasn't* come.

Silence.

EUGENIA (*by the window*). Sssh. (*Pause.*) You realise we have no idea what is going on out there. None. We can only stand here, and wait for what is coming. I often think something is about to come out of the silence at us, suddenly appear down the line.

POLYA. Remember those corpses in the ditch by the dacha — all squashed up at one end with those hundreds of butterflies fluttering on top of them, murdered by bandits. I'll never forget those faces, their mouths open, one of the heads was sliced in half.

EUGENIA. I don't just mean the bandits and if they attack . . . (*She turns.*) So many things may have changed *without us knowing,* Polya. (*Pause.*) Our street in Moscow will be completely different — it could have been torn down, they may be using it as barracks, soldiers sleeping in our bedrooms, or the apartment may have been swallowed up by Government offices, (*Slight smile.*) the Transport Department, my old room full of bus routes, and filing cabinets in the bathroom . . . And the language will be changing, how you address people in the street, if I met somebody I used to know, have coffee with, this will sound stupid, but I start wondering what would

I do, what would I call her? . . . What should I say? (*Pause.*)
We are so ignorant, Polya. (*She turns.*) I am. It terrifies me
sometimes. (*Suddenly breathing into the speaking tube:*)
Vastly ignorant. (*She looks up. Pause.*) The Master will never
discuss his work with us and nor should we expect it.

POLYA. No?

EUGENIA. But Polya have you any idea why we have heard
nothing from the authorities?

Pause.

POLYA. Madame — I think there is something you ought to see.

She moves towards NIKOLAI's *private space.*

EUGENIA (*hesitating*). What — we have to go in there?

POLYA (*turning to face her*). I found these — I didn't know
whether to show you.

POLYA *is pushing her hand down the side of* NIKOLAI's *bed,
bringing out handfuls of large pristine white official letters
with the Government seal on them.*

EUGENIA. They're not all official letters are they — and none of
them opened? He must have opened some of them?

POLYA. Not one.

*She is producing letters from every crack and corner, from
behind lamps, from under the bunks, from behind the stove.*

EUGENIA. The Master never forgets anything — he didn't open
these *deliberately.*

POLYA (*scrambling on the top bunk, and near the roof*). There
are plenty more, even under his sheets! These are the worst I
think. (*She comes down with more.*) Telegrams . . .

EUGENIA. Because I'm not allowed to collect the mail, Polya — I
had no idea these had come.

POLYA *hands her the red-bound envelopes.* EUGENIA *stares
down at them.*

What do you think they all say — what do you think they
want?

POLYA. We could open them, Madame.

EUGENIA. Open his letters! If he found out . . .

Silence. Suddenly pushing them into POLYA's *hand, nervous smile.*

You open them. No, you can't read can you Polya?

POLYA. Not quite.

EUGENIA. Give them back. I'm not that much of a coward! I'll do my own dirty work.

POLYA *crosses herself as* EUGENIA *opens the telegrams and reads them out.*

URGENT. MUST HAVE *NEWS*, DETAILS TELEPHONE EXAMINER IMMEDIATELY. WHAT PROGRESS?

POLYA *tears open another and gives it to* EUGENIA.

WHY NO NEWS? REPORT STATE OF WORK WITHOUT DELAY. MOST URGENT. REPLY ESSENTIAL. (*Looking at* POLYA.) I think we get the idea. (*Staring at the other envelopes.*) I hope they don't get even worse.

POLYA. They better go back.

She starts hastily pushing letters back into cracks.

EUGENIA. God knows what else there is we don't know about.

POLYA. Well, Madame — if you really want to see.

She looks at EUGENIA *as she pushes the letters back.*

EUGENIA (*quiet*). You better show me everything, Polya.

POLYA. There's this, the official ledger the Master has to keep. (*Indicating the huge bulky volume.*) There is not a word in it, it's completely bare.

EUGENIA (*opening the huge ledger*). Not one entry? About the long trip he made with Sasha. (*Staring.*) All these blank pages!

POLYA. And this is the most serious.

EUGENIA. Why?

POLYA (*indicating the bags of money from the drawer*). He's spent some of the money, he's spent over half I think.

EUGENIA. And there is no record of it? (*She moves in agitation.*)
He must have spent it on all those things he brought back for
his work — and the food he bribed off people to feed us with.
I wondered how on earth he'd got it. I didn't dare ask.
(*Sharper:*) I didn't want to know.

POLYA. None of it is railway business — whichever way you look
at it.

EUGENIA (*facing her*). No, Polya. If he's misappropriated
government funds that could be disastrous — if it was
discovered, even the Master could be . . . (*She stops.*) even
he . . .

Pause.

POLYA. The Master could get shot, yes.

EUGENIA (*sharper*). It's almost certain. (*She turns.*) You mustn't
mention any of this, Polya, that we've seen . . .

*A noise at the door; they bolt across the carriage back to their
places, as the door opens and* SASHA *enters.*

EUGENIA (*shouts*). It's you, Sasha — you shouldn't give us
shocks like that. (*Really loud:*) What do you think you're
doing? Why didn't you knock? Don't you ever do that again!

POLYA (*by the window looking out*). Where's the Master? He's
not right outside anymore . . .

SASHA (*standing still*). I haven't seen him. I've been walking
down the line by myself.

EUGENIA. Sasha — I have to ask you something serious, are you
listening carefully?

SASHA (*watching closely from the wall*). What is it?

EUGENIA. Tell me what your father is doing? (*Pause.*) When you
went off with him on that long journey for all those months —
what did he tell you?

Pause.

SASHA. He didn't tell me anything.

POLYA. I don't think that's true. (*Looking straight at him.*)
You're lying, Sasha.

EUGENIA. We're here in the middle of the country and your father is doing all this work with Polya. Why?

SASHA *is watching them.*

POLYA. Did he talk to you about his work? Yes or no?

SASHA (*quiet*). I think he did.

EUGENIA. Sasha — I realise we're not meant to know, normally I wouldn't ask. But you have to tell me, it could prove very dangerous to all of us if you keep it to yourself.

SASHA. He told me everything he was doing.

POLYA. He did?

SASHA (*slowly*). But I was so scared while he was telling me, I was so frightened — I don't remember what he said . . . only that it's important. I can't even remember where we went.

EUGENIA. Sasha — is that true?

POLYA. I don't believe it.

SASHA. Yes! I realised hours afterwards I couldn't remember what secret he told me.

EUGENIA. You can't even remember a part of it?

SASHA. Nothing.

EUGENIA (*suddenly moving*). One thing is certain, sooner or later somebody is going to follow these up, they are going to seek us out, to find what has happened. They'll burst in here one day, and that will probably be the end of all this.

POLYA. And us as well — probably.

EUGENIA. Yes. (*Looking at them.*) And we can't escape anywhere, obviously — they will come after us. So . . . (*She moves, picks up a letter.*) we've got to reply to these, (*Pause.*) write letters on his behalf and put something in here, Polya. (*She indicates the official ledger.*) Somehow we've got to discover Railway details, make up false records, fill up this with what he's discovered on his trip, so it appears he's made an effort.

POLYA. Give them something to read! (*She moves.*) How are we going to do it?

EUGENIA. I don't know — have to try to remember the geography my governess taught me, my schooling, towns and small places in the northern district, all the bits that were always the most boring. (*She moves.*) Maybe we'll find a map among his private papers we can use.

POLYA. I'll go through them.

EUGENIA. We have to lie, Polya — lies that won't be too specific, too obvious, about the things we found — (*She corrects herself.*) — that the Master found, 'in such and such a place some progress was noticed, the workers conscientious'. Maybe they will take so long to check with the northern depot — communications can't be good at the moment — that when they find out, it won't matter so much by then. (*Looking at the ledger.*) We're living on explosive leaving this blank.

POLYA. Do you know anything about the Northern Railway, Madame — I don't.

EUGENIA. No, or telephones. But we'll have to use our imagination — (*Self-mocking smile.*) — if I have any. We invent if necessary.

Lifting the pen from the desk towards the virgin white pages, she writes.

'Day one, departed.' (*As she writes:*) The Master must not know anything about this of course, he would tear it all out at once. We're just helping him because he's so very busy.

POLYA. Who are we more afraid of, Madame, him or them?

EUGENIA (*sharper*). Polya — you shouldn't talk like that. (*Looking down.*) What do you think the penalties are for doing this — they may be worse than for not doing anything at all.

NIKOLAI is standing in the doorway; EUGENIA starts, closes the ledger and moves across the carriage, holding it behind her.

There you are — I was wondering where you were.

NIKOLAI is not even looking at her.

NIKOLAI. I thought you must have stopped, Polya. What happened to you?

He stares down at POLYA *who is dripping with sweat, her hair matted back.*

POLYA (*looking at him, then away*). I had to have a rest, Barin — so I am taking one . . .

NIKOLAI. So it appears. (*Pause.*) Did we agree it was time to stop?

POLYA (*quiet*). No, Barin.

EUGENIA. Nikolai, I want to ask you — have you had any messages from Moscow, any letters or telegrams from the authorities?

NIKOLAI. From Moscow? Not of any significance. (*He turns back to* POLYA.) Polya, time is important to us, interruptions will prove very damaging. We are involved in a race against time.

POLYA (*very quiet*). But I needed to have a break.

NIKOLAI. Of course. I don't want you to be over-worked, Polya. If it has been a strain, then, certainly you must take a pause; we will start again in one and a half minutes.

POLYA (*suddenly*). When I am ready Nikolai Semenovitch, we will go on, not before.

Startled pause.

EUGENIA (*worried by her boldness*). Polya . . .

POLYA (*facing him*). I am so hot, I am filthy. Look at me.

NIKOLAI (*very firm, all his authority*). I need you to do it Polya. (*Watching her defiant face.*) You can have all my rations for the rest of the week, in return for more work tonight.

POLYA. I don't think you should try to bribe me, either. And you must not interfere with the ration allocation, Barin — it will put the accounts in an even worse mess and we'll go back to starving.

Silence. She faces him.

NIKOLAI. She disobeys me — and she threatens me. (*Lightly.*) And I cannot dismiss her — because there is no obvious replacement waiting outside. (*Sharper.*) We will resume in less than a minute.

POLYA. Nikolai Semenovitch, when I go on — it will be because I want to and because Sasha says it's important, what you're doing, though he hasn't been able to tell us what it is.

NIKOLAI. What I do *is* important, naturally. I wouldn't ask people to waste their time.

POLYA (*nervously, but staring straight at him*). Are you going to tell me what it is, Barin?

NIKOLAI. Your break for a rest is now over.

POLYA. I believe it *is* something important. But I would like to know what . . . what I am doing this for, Barin.

NIKOLAI (*ignoring this*). We must go on now. (*Sharp.*) Polya, I have to have your help — I can't do without it.

POLYA *stares at him.*

POLYA. I know that. If I do it — it will be in my own time, (*With great dignity she kneels before the tube.*) which may be now, for a strictly *limited* time. (*Sharp:*) You better go back to where you should be, Barin — or you'll be losing the time you've got me for.

She begins to sing, on her knees, into the tube, a loud, piercing, powerful song.

Blackout.

Scene Four

SASHA *is alone in the carriage, a distant sound of guns, the outside world encroaching. There is grumbling gunfire, for the moment in the distance, sniping and occasionally the much larger sound of a field gun going off, shells falling — the noise is sporadic. SASHA is sitting at the far end of the carriage, holding one of the pistols and pointing it straight at the door. There is a sudden, much louder sound of calls and shouts right outside the door, excited cries. SASHA stands holding the gun out in front of him, pointing at the door.*

SASHA. Who is that? (*Pulling back the catch on the gun.*) Who is out there? I warn you — I am *armed*.

EUGENIA and POLYA burst through door, hair untidy. Distant gunfire behind them in the night.

EUGENIA. What are you doing pointing that thing at us Sasha . . . ?

SASHA. I didn't know who was out there. (*Very real apprehension.*) You never know what could come in from out there — especially on a night like this.

EUGENIA and POLYA are licking meat fat off their hands, having been cooking outside. There is a new earthiness and directness in their manner to each other.

EUGENIA. Do you think we burnt it? (*Glancing back through the door.*) It looks like we may have burnt it!

POLYA. I'd completely forgotten the taste of meat — there're some things you could almost commit murder for, aren't there! (*Licking fingers.*) If only the comrade from Moscow had brought more of it.

EUGENIA. Took so long to pluck them — I had to restrain myself from just tearing the birds apart — (*A last lick.*) — little sputters of blood going everywhere — my cooking is so rudimentary Polya.

POLYA. They won't notice.

EUGENIA (*suddenly*). What are we doing? We're not ready! We have to prepare the table, they could be back any moment.

SASHA. Papa's not going to make us all sit down to eat, is he? He can't hold a dinner party during a battle.

EUGENIA. Of course — something small like that is certainly not going to stop him. If I could think of any possible way of preventing him I would do it, it's not exactly what we want the Commissar of Labour to see.

POLYA and EUGENIA run around the carriage and produce a beautiful white table cloth from the drawers under the bunks, silver candle sticks and cutlery, fine quality china. During the following exchanges the table is prepared to its full splendour and the candles lit, the gunfire in the distance beginning to roll towards them.

EUGENIA (*hearing the field gun*). Remember those nights in the apartment the first days of the Revolution, Polya, hearing the noise, just like this.

POLYA. The night everyone ran for shelter from the guns to the hotel across the street, during dinner.

EUGENIA. You were carrying all the luggage we could snatch in the time, weren't you? I piled you with so much silver you could hardly move. (*Imitates* POLYA's *tottering figure*.) You lurched down the stairs like this.

POLYA. Yes, silver was dropping behind me all the way down the street — if I tried to pick it up, I just dropped more . . .

EUGENIA. And the passage of the hotel filled with all those men keeping their hats on all night, walking up and down standing guard on us, everyone of them dressed like the Master.

POLYA. Yes, but not quite as well.

EUGENIA. Hundreds and hundreds of them squashed into the corridor, I came out in the night and there was just this sea of bobbing black hats.

POLYA (*laying the silver round the table*). And the cavalry officer, remember him, Madame, what was he called? The one that sheltered in our room the next afternoon for a rest. I had to tie his tie for him when he woke, he'd never tied it for himself — he crawled out of the hotel during the shelling.

EUGENIA. And the Master demanding where room service was.

The gunfire becomes a little louder.

SASHA. Is it nearer?

EUGENIA. God, I've forgotten half of it already — those extraordinary faces staring at me . . .

POLYA (*moving around the carriage lighting all the candles*). Perfect strangers kept on giving me orders, pushing messages into my hand, and saying, 'Just run along the passage for me to such and such a room.'

EUGENIA. If I'd known what it meant — I would have remembered it more. I knew things wouldn't be the same again, but I just had a sense of total irritation all the time constantly being kept awake, the firing, like somebody kicking you in the ankles all the time, so you're in a terrible nervy temper — feelings hardly matching the size of the occasion and how near we were. (*Sharp.*) How inadequate one's immediate responses often are, mine anyway. (*She moves. Loud:*) Was that them? Are we ready?

POLYA. Sasha put that gun away . . . No, hide it properly, not there, that's the most obvious place.

SASHA *had put it under his pillow. He now puts it behind the stove.*

EUGENIA. Polya, we have to do everything in our power, and I mean everything, to make sure the Commissar of Labour doesn't interrogate the Master. Steer him away from anything about railway business. And we can't let him mention his work.

POLYA. Yes. (*Kicking the tube into a corner.*) If he sees anything, we say it's part of the heating system.

Pause.

EUGENIA. You know if we got the food in here now, and we were able to move this carriage on our own, we could ride off with all this for ourselves, slide off down the line away from danger . . .

VERKOFF *enters with* NIKOLAI. VERKOFF *is flushed from watching the gun battle. As* NIKOLAI *takes off his coat, we see he is formally dressed for dinner.*

NIKOLAI. They are waiting to feed us.

VERKOFF. We should be safe in here. (*To* EUGENIA:) I hope I'm right, you look concerned. What a night! We got quite close to the action didn't we Nikolai Semenovitch, caught glimpses of them through the trees!

NIKOLAI (*calmly*). I saw nothing, the smoke got in my eyes.

SASHA. Who are they fighting?

VERKOFF. They are flushing out some white bandits. Some renegade soldiers, and a collection of bandits have teamed up, a really seedy bunch! But they've got themselves three old guns somehow, and are roaming the forest. (*Gunfire. He smiles.*) Shouldn't be many of them left by morning.

NIKOLAI (*staring down at the table*). There are no table napkins, Polya — for some reason they have been forgotten.

POLYA *rushes for them as* NIKOLAI *pours wine.*

This is the best bottle I have left, it may be a little thin.

VERKOFF (*looking around*). What have you done to this place? Railway life seems to be suiting you comrade!

NIKOLAI. Despite the monstrous administrative error — a little progress has been possible.

VERKOFF. What monstrous error is that?

EUGENIA. Polya! You better bring the food at once — (*Sharp:*) — as quickly as you can.

POLYA *exits with a silver tray.*

NIKOLAI (*charming smile*). What you have singularly failed to rectify. Do not be fooled by the appearance of luxury — you have left us in a corner where even the peasants do not live . . . When it rains you can hear the rats squealing and scuffling underneath; some of them poke their heads through to peer at me. (*Slight smile.*) And they are free and I am caged.

The sound of guns, all the time slightly nearer.

VERKOFF. Don't worry — they won't be able to shoot straight. (*Looking at* NIKOLAI's *table.*) If they could see what was going on inside a Government train!

POLYA *comes in with the food — small roasted pieces of some bird, scattered across a large silver platter. The amount of meat is tiny on the huge tray.*

EUGENIA (*nervous*). Here's the food, Comrade.

VERKOFF. And we're going to be eating it off English silver?

NIKOLAI. Of course, it's English.

VERKOFF. Only the best naturally!

NIKOLAI (*charming smile*). I have never been rich enough to afford to buy anything but the best.

POLYA *is dividing the meat up, the smell of freshly roasted game filling the stage.*

(*Unabashed*:) In England you find quality everywhere. An immensely civilized, comfortable place — arriving there is like sliding into a warm bath (*He stares at* VERKOFF.) which nobody is suddenly going to try to empty. People never argue there, the clothes are beautifully made, the service superb.

The food is now ready in front of them.

VERKOFF (*staring at him, suddenly very loud*). Nikolai Semenovitch you are the biggest snob I have *ever* met and I have met a few. (*Pointing at him.*) It's shameless! And it gets *worse* with him!

EUGENIA (*hastily*). My husband finds it difficult to break old habits.

VERKOFF. The way you dress! Even here where nobody at all can see you — a Jew that behaves like a Grand Duke, who had to be the best-dressed man in Moscow. Someone that can serve a meal like this on his family silver in the middle of a forest, during a battle!

NIKOLAI. If the mind is to function it has to be looked after. It's as simple as that.

VERKOFF (*sharp smile*). You know you could antagonise certain people behaving like this, it has been known! (*Looking straight at him.*) It's as well you've been employed on railway business isn't it?

EUGENIA *looks at* POLYA. VERKOFF *points at* NIKOLAI's *feet. Really loud.*

I shouldn't think there's another pair of shoes left like that in the whole of Russia!

NIKOLAI. Comrade — I thought you had a revolution so you

would be able to dress like me — not I like you.

They look at VERKOFF. *Silence, followed by a sudden loud laugh.*

VERKOFF. Did you hear him? (*Pause.*) People have been shot for saying less.

The sound of shelling, growing gradually closer all the time.

NIKOLAI. I don't necessarily disapprove of everything that has happened (*Indicating himself.*) though of course a mistake like this should have been avoided. Despite that — the astronomical incompetence that was allowed before, that was freely tolerated, it amazes me now.

VERKOFF (*sharp*). He admits that much.

NIKOLAI (*incisive*). Before it happened there was an unhelpful nervousness too — a general unease, people hurrying faster between the front door and their carriage, myself included.

VERKOFF. He had to run into his house!

NIKOLAI. Yes, a listlessness when in public places (*Slight smile.*) . . . Waiters became unpredictable. (*Pause.*) There was a constant sensation of something pressing, pressing down on one like a weight on the walls — needless to say I was completely unaware of it until everything 'erupted' . . . then quite suddenly I realised it had been there all the time.

SASHA (*suddenly really loud, famished*). Papa — *please* can we start, aren't we going to eat now! We've been *waiting* to eat this — I can't wait any more, please let us begin.

Silence.

NIKOLAI. Sasha. (*His manner is truly formidable, dangerous.*) What is the meaning of this? Have you forgotten there are guests present? (*Pause.*) Remove yourself to your room and eat there . . . and take a knife and fork, I will not have you not eating properly, you are not to eat with your bare hands.

NIKOLAI *turns back to the table.*

Let us begin.

Everybody falls on their food violently except for NIKOLAI.

There is no hurry, the food will not run away.

The gunfire is getting nearer.

VERKOFF. We want to eat before we die! (*Tearing at the meat furiously.*) My family were all butchers you know.

EUGENIA *looks nervous.*

But they all hated meat. (*Looking up.*) If I'd known you were hungry I would have brought some more . . .

EUGENIA *tries to resist eating with her fingers.* POLYA *sitting separate, pulling meat up to her mouth. A sound comes out of her, a crying noise. She curls her body to the wall.*

EUGENIA. What is it, Polya − are you all right?

POLYA. Oh yes − it's just slightly good. (*She makes a deep famished cry again.*) Just a little nice, you know.

The gunfire is now very close. VERKOFF *looks at* NIKOLAI *presiding over the table.*

VERKOFF (*with relish*). Look at him now! I would love to see the shock people have as you go about your railway business − that I would pay to see. (*Loud.*) I would queue to see it!

EUGENIA (*nervous*). Have some more wine, Comrade, here . . .

VERKOFF (*loud, moving around, his fingers stabbing out*). They have started sending our special trains from Moscow with performing groups on them, young people, actors, musicians, spreading across the country, explaining, informing, communicating − the idea of *them* passing *you* at some remote station, it is wonderful. Rolling back the door of the carriage and finding this apparition − this figure looking as if he's stepped out of the last century, if not before, dressed for going to the opera, waving his stick at them and shouting, go away, don't interrupt me, I am too busy, my work is vital!

NIKOLAI. Why should it be extraordinary?

VERKOFF. I love the idea! (*Sharp look.*) What rich times these are, eh, Nikolai Semenovitch!

NIKOLAI (*calmly*). It is only children and government officials that can't hold two totally separate − seemingly opposing −

ideas in their head at the same time.

A shell breaks closer to the carriage as the battle rolls towards them. EUGENIA *and* SASHA *instinctively duck.*

NIKOLAI (*calmly*). I am engaged in a struggle where the outcome can never be totally guaranteed — but it is a reasonable prediction to make that this carriage will become as famous as the one they signed the German surrender in, and we are by coincidence also in a forest.

The noise of sniper fire is suddenly closer as well.

(*Glancing at* VERKOFF:) If I do what I am capable of — this, my appointment, will be the highlight of your career.

VERKOFF (*broad smile*). As Telephone Examiner!

NIKOLAI (*lightly*). You will be erecting plaques on this wall in years to come and showing your grandchildren. People will be coming here to inspect where it was all done (*Charming smile.*) though for the convenience of the public they may wish to move the carriage nearer to civilisation.

The loud whistle of a shell seemingly descending directly above them hangs in the air for a second, as the battle reaches them.

VERKOFF. Careful! They're getting really close. Take cover!

POLYA, SASHA *and* EUGENIA *move over to the bunks,* VERKOFF *crouches; only* NIKOLAI *remains sitting absolutely erect as the shell explodes directly behind the carriage, a bright white flash behind the window. The walls of the carriage shake violently. The wine falls over, spreading a huge red satin over the tablecloth and dripping down the side.*

NIKOLAI *still sits absolutely erect.*

NIKOLAI (*calmly, seriously*). I can assure you my friend — the modern world is grinding around in this carriage, forcing its way out, coming into existence right here, but any disturbance now does not help.

The loud whine of a second shell descending.

I'd appreciate them being reduced to a minimum.

The shell explodes behind the carriage.

Having to operate surrounded by one's family . . . women and children, is a problem.

Silence. A pause in the bombardment. POLYA *and* EUGENIA *look up from the bunk.*

VERKOFF (*up again, moving sharply around the carriage*). It has stopped for the moment. I must get my inspection over before it starts again.

EUGENIA. What inspection is that Comrade — I thought you'd seen everything you'd come to see.

VERKOFF. The official records of course. Where has our money been going?

EUGENIA (*sharp*). Money?

VERKOFF (*to* NIKOLAI). Until recently we were not getting any replies from you to any of our messages.

NIKOLAI. I was not aware I had replied at all.

VERKOFF (*rifling through the papers on the desk*). How were they all? I haven't seen them for months. How is Varyov, the one with half a moustache, and the little squat ugly one, who always has his flies open, what's his name? At the depot? How have you been getting on with him?

NIKOLAI. I will not conceal facts, I cannot lie to you, I have never been to the depot.

POLYA (*moving across the carriage with the huge volume*). Here is the ledger — all the records we have, comrade, are *here.*

NIKOLAI. I can save you wasting your time.

EUGENIA. Nikolai, you must move from there, the wine's dripping. Why don't you come here?

POLYA *crosses herself as* VERKOFF *flicks the pages of the ledger.*

VERKOFF (*flicking, reading*). 'Progress considerable' . . . 'work satisfactory' . . . 'tolerable progress' . . . This is such an extensive record. (*Strides.*) Places I had forgotten existed. (*He turns a page.*) Places I've never heard of — you have been conscientious Comrade! I must keep this.

EUGENIA (*sharp*). Keep it? Why comrade?

VERKOFF (*sharp smile*). To study, to read at nights. (*Slamming the ledger shut.*)

NIKOLAI. You must show me, you must let me see this, there's been a mistake, I wouldn't wish you to leave here with a false impression.

The gunfire is further off again now, to the side of the carriage.

VERKOFF. I must go — I must leave while I can still get out.

EUGENIA. Yes, Comrade.

VERKOFF (*suddenly really loud, volatile smile, full of relish*). You're an impossible man, Nikolai Semenovitch — what an absurd creation we have here. What an infuriating bastard.

He is moving around, his powerful body seeming to fill the carriage.

And he flaunts it!

He suddenly physically lifts NIKOLAI up off the ground in a single movement and holds him like an enormous doll.

He revels in it. (*Holding him.*) He's got 'made at the Ritz' stamped on his arse. He has! I can feel the crest right here.

NIKOLAI (*calm, great authority*). Put me down, Comrade.

VERKOFF (*carrying straight on*). Hang you up on this peg as an exhibit in your own carriage — an item for future generations to wonder at.

He puts NIKOLAI down and points.

This is the man I made Telephone Examiner, see! I did! (*Moving — very loud.*) I will tell you this my friend, I will never forget you — I will *not* forget you.

NIKOLAI. Somebody else said that to me recently.

VERKOFF. Has that penetrated that thin skull — gone all the way down?

Suddenly his tone changes, as he produces an envelope from his pocket. Serious.

You have new orders now. Their contents will not surprise you, I think. Read them and goodbye.

NIKOLAI (*seeing* VERKOFF *at the door*). I must accompany you, then.

VERKOFF (*to* EUGENIA). He wants to escort me off his 'estate'!

Gunfire in the distance.

Come on then before it's too late.

He goes.

EUGENIA (*loud*). Kolia!

NIKOLAI *turns in the doorway.*

You will be careful, don't say any more — just let him go. Leave him.

Silence.

NIKOLAI. Am I to understand you are giving me instructions . . .?

EUGENIA. No, I'm just warning you. I mean . . . (*Looking down.*)

NIKOLAI. There are obviously things going on here — things you have done, Eugenia, that I do not know about. (*Pause. He looks at her.*) We will discuss them when I return. (*He goes.*)

POLYA (*turns, stares across at* EUGENIA). Eugenia Michailovna. (*Slight pause.*) We did it!

EUGENIA. I don't know . . . I couldn't tell . . .

POLYA (*very excited*). We did, we did!

She physically catches hold of EUGENIA, *squeezing her arm.*

We've *survived* the visit, haven't we . . . we made it work, we've managed it.

EUGENIA. Yes . . .

POLYA. God, every time he looked round, though, the Comrade Commissar, my heart started going like this — I'd rather have been out there where the guns are going off. (*She looks at* EUGENIA.) We did all right, didn't we?

EUGENIA. I hope so . . . (*Suddenly urgent*:) Polya, you'd better go after the Master, I think; we can't take the chance, keep by his side, don't let him explain anything.

POLYA. I'll catch them. (*Running across the carriage to grab her shawl.*) I'll talk non-stop, gabble all the way to the Comrade's car. Nobody else will get a word in . . .

POLYA goes. EUGENIA and SASHA are alone — the huge red wine stain dripping off the tablecloth, the charred chewed bones of the bird spread across the tablecloth.

EUGENIA (*urgent*). Have we managed it, Sasha?

SASHA. Mama?

EUGENIA (*moving across the carriage*). The orders? (*Sharp.*) Where are the new orders?

She tears open the envelope.

We're being moved at once to Moscow.

She stares at the paper.

In this carriage. They're sending a locomotive to take us across country at night, next week.

SASHA. What does that mean? Is it bad news? (*Watching her.*) What are they going to do with us?

EUGENIA. That's all it says. (*Very quiet.*) We are going to be met at Moscow. (*She moves across the carriage.*)

SASHA (*worried*). By whom, mama?

EUGENIA (*moving, thinking*). We could have all died on several occasions over these past months because of your father — left to his own devices that might have happened . . . Have we helped him or not? *Did I do the right thing?* (*Surprised at herself.*) Without even asking him! I wish I knew more. Will he ever let me help him again if I have the chance?

SASHA. What do you think will happen in Moscow?

EUGENIA. There is no telling. (*Louder, very strong.*) We mustn't lose the protection of being here Sasha — we must fight to keep it, the protection of his job, I am *not* going back to starving, chewing nuts crawling on one's knees licking the ground.

The sound of gunfire suddenly louder again.

If we lose this, if we're thrown off here, we don't all survive. It's as simple as that. (*She turns sharper.*) What are all those things he talked about . . . grinding around in this carriage . . . modern . . . going to be the highlight of people's lives. What did he mean?

SASHA. I don't know mama.

EUGENIA (*suddenly*). I am going to find out what he's doing. Private space or no private space — I have to know.

She pulls the partition down around his part of the carriage.

Why haven't I done this before. (*Pulling out his drawers.*) What am I hunting for? Will he have written it down. Will it suddenly be here, staring at me. (*She pulls open the cases.*) Tell me — do you feel different, Sasha?

SASHA. What do you mean mama?

EUGENIA. What do you think different means?

EUGENIA *is emptying* NIKOLAI's *drawers and pulling open all his hidden places, her mood excited.*

(*Going through his papers. Lightly.*) You know Sasha, my whole adult life, every waking moment seems to have belonged to your papa . . . his world, his determination, the power of his moods.

Another piece of furniture is upturned.

So where is it? What *is* his work Sasha, where's the answer?

SASHA (*watching her from a distance*). I *told* you, I don't know, mama.

EUGENIA (*excited as a flare goes up outside the window*). Oh if only he'd let me do something, your father, — let me do more, *let me.*

She is framed in the light of the flare, sensual energy.

What is happening to us Sasha? What is happening to me?

She turns powerfully towards SASHA.

You don't like me talking like this . . . do you?

SASHA. No, mama, it's alright.

SASHA *watches her closely.*

EUGENIA. It's because you have never heard it before. Not used to it.

She moves towards him.

You look older, Sasha . . . (*Touching his face.*) Is that hair, a beard, there's a man growing here.

She returns to NIKOLAI's *belongings that she has strewn across the stage, she pulls out of the last pigskin case, a camera, bulky film camera, smothered in dust.*

Just an old camera! That can't be it. He hasn't used it since we arrived in here. It's covered in dust. (*She blows dust off the camera.*)

SASHA (*staring down at the camera, pushes it with his foot*). Is it possible, do you think, for somebody to have new ideas; somebody who never goes out, never talks about it to anyone. (*Watching her.*) Is that possible? Somebody who can't boil a kettle.

EUGENIA. Who can't boil a kettle?

SASHA. Nobody . . . no-one.

The noise of a shell whistling and screaming down towards them, exploding behind the carriage.

That was very close. They're coming back!

EUGENIA *snuffs out some of the candles and pulls* SASHA *towards her, in the middle of the carriage. Her mood is strangely excited.*

EUGENIA. You should remember tonight, Sasha — write it down, we've constantly been on the edge of great events, do you realise, just outside, in Moscow and here on the edge of a battle, so near we've been able to smell them. (*Facing him.*) You will remember it for me? You will?

SASHA. Yes, mama.

EUGENIA. Better than you have been? We both will.

SASHA (*staring at her as the shells begin to fall*). I had a dream about papa earlier today — they tore off his clothes and tied him to a gate in a field and shot him in the head. Do you think we're going to be alright — or are they going to try to kill us (*Staring at her.*).

Pause.

EUGENIA. Do your dreams often come true?

SASHA (*pause*). Yes.

EUGENIA. Let it not be for a while, then. (*Slight smile.*) Not quite yet. (*Touching him.*) You never know we may be lucky.

Fade.

ACT TWO

January, 1924

Scene One

*The carriage. Cold, snow outside, the sound of the rail shunting
yards. A military band can be heard rehearsing in the distance,
stopping and starting, sudden, dissonant, edgy noise; silence, then
rapid brassy playing, sometimes ceremonial, sometimes mournful,
little spiky bursts sporadically heard through the scene as the
musicians rehearse. We do not hear the main tune of the piece
they are playing in its entirety.*

*The carriage is full of steam, clothes hanging up to dry, towels,
sheets and other clothes including underwear drying on the
bunks, and hanging from the ceiling. There is a much more
informal look to the grandness of the carriage, piles of apples,
carrots, and potatoes, and other food stored, kitchen utensils
hanging up.*

*POLYA is pouring hot water from a large white china jug.
EUGENIA, dressed only in her petticoat, kneeling by an enamel
bath, is having her neck washed, steam pouring from the jug as
hot water slops into the bath. SASHA, dressed in plain clothes
and looking older, is pacing the carriage learning something from
a book.*

EUGENIA (*mock terror*). Stop it, Polya, stop! It's too hot you're
going to boil me alive . . . don't — (*Screams as if scalded.*)
Don't! See, I'm going scarlet.

POLYA (*standing over bath*). Don't you dare move till I've
finished.

EUGENIA (*shrieking in half-mock pain as water falls onto her arms*). Polya, it hurts, you've never known such pain! For goodness' sake stop . . .

POLYA (*smiles*). You're not going to move till I tell you to.

EUGENIA. I'm going to be late, you realise, terribly late, and I can't be today. (*Getting up, laughing.*) You're going to let me go. (EUGENIA *gets up.*)

POLYA. What's so special about today?

EUGENIA *shivers furiously, her bare shoulders shaking. During the following exchanges, she dresses at a furious rate, pulling on heavy socks and shoes, a plain black skirt, a brown sweater and at the end a long great coat — she is totally transformed.*

SASHA (*pacing up and down the carriage trying desperately to memorise facts*). The Moscow drainage system is now the envy of the world . . . the weight of refuse now being dealt with has increased by six times in as many years. (*He looks at his notes.*) No, four times, . . . cutting through the old foundations of the city . . . the new drainage boasts three million, is it three millions . . .?

Jarring notes of the music outside.

POLYA (*shouts out of the window*). Play in tune, can't you! (*Turning.*) If we have to have a band just out there — why can't they play something a bit better? (*Looking at* EUGENIA.) Why are you rushing so much?

EUGENIA. We start making the new Railway Timetables today — and we have to notify all the regions of the new ticket price, it's going to be a rush to make the deadline.

POLYA (*sharp smile*). Sounds as if it can wait five minutes to me.

EUGENIA. It's an office full of men. I'm the *only* woman there still — so I have to be on time. (*She smiles as she dresses.*) The whole of that building smells of men.

POLYA. Bring some of them back here sometime!

EUGENIA (*fast, smiling*). I'm getting a little less afraid of them. They keep on wanting to know where I come from, really curious about us having the tiny apartment but also being allowed to keep this. (*Indicates the carriage.*) They want all my personal history. I give them a little bit at a time.

POLYA. At the mail sorting office we've got a miserable collection of males at the moment. People just 'passing through' . . . (*She smiles.*) Means a lot of wandering hands! (*Suddenly shrieks with laughter.*) But *nobody* discovered about my reading, you were right, how basic it was, (*Loud:*) deeply basic at the start. Me peering at letters, hopefully throwing them in the right holes, letters going off in all directions. If people had bad handwriting they didn't stand a chance with me!

EUGENIA (*teasing smile*). To think some letters travelling *two thousand* miles and then having to end up with you, Polya!

POLYA. Now I'm really efficient — there isn't enough post to keep me quiet. (*Sombre noise outside the window.*) Shut up!

SASHA (*testing himself*). At the deepest point in the drainage system — how deep is it?

POLYA. Sasha, what on earth are you doing?

SASHA. It's another school dissertation, you could either write about a member of your family — or an aspect of Moscow.

EUGENIA (*incredulous*). And you chose the drains?

SASHA. I deliberately picked an unpopular subject so I was bound to do well — I mean nobody knows anything about the city drainage system and what's found in it, I'm certain none of the teachers do.

EUGENIA (*slight smile*). And what about your family, does nobody know about them?

SASHA (*hesitates for a split second*). No . . .

EUGENIA (*moving very fast, putting her scarf on*). I'll probably kill myself, won't I, going from being that hot into that cold; it's really snowing, but I *will* not be late. Where's my identity card? (*Moving.*) I haven't seen Nikolai for days, it seems . . . (*By the door as she pulls it open.*) Come on! Head down and charge.

She goes out into the cold.

POLYA (*calling after her, as she pushes the door shut*). Don't run in the snow, you'll fall on your arse. (*Loud, smile.*) You will anyway.

POLYA *closes the door, as the band plays a burst of music.*

What an unearthly noise! Why do you think they're rehearsing that sort of music? . . .

SASHA (*by the window, jumping up*). I can't see them. Just out of sight, as usual! There've been a lot of comings and goings . . . soldiers arriving by train last night, cars moving across the shunting yard.

POLYA. Yes, I heard officials from all over the country had been arriving since early this morning. I think something has happened.

POLYA *looks across the width of the carriage at him.*

Now – for you, Sasha. Do you need a wash? Very definitely I should think.

SASHA (*in a strangely adult manner*). Do I?

POLYA. Ages since I washed you. (*Something stops her.*) I don't think I even ought to try now.

SASHA (*pulling his top off, washing himself*). No – I don't think so.

POLYA (*sharp smile*). You used to call for me with that noise, used to bray for me, remember? 'Pol-ya' – that's how it went.

SASHA (*lightly*). You were always slow in answering, too.

POLYA (*doing the call*). 'Pol-yaa make my bed' . . . 'wash me' or in the middle of the night 'I'm afraid, come to me quick, I'm frightened of the demon with three heads.'

SASHA. What demons? I was stupidly over-sensitive. (*Looking at her, slight smile.*) When you came to me, bent over the bed, you had that particular smell – I've always been meaning to tell you.

POLYA (*loud*). What smell?

SASHA. The cheese smell of course — all those days you did it, and it stayed with you.

POLYA (*loud*). Did what?

SASHA (*teasingly*). When you carried cheese — before we found you and brought you to Moscow. You coming to the house from the village wearing that long black dress, so long it scraped the ground, carrying those horrible curd cheeses; that smell was always there.

POLYA (*angry, loud*). You're not trying to tell me, Sasha, it's still there!

SASHA. Maybe.

POLYA (*moving towards him*). You rude little bastard. Come here.

SASHA. You haven't got a hope of catching me anymore.

They circle each other.

POLYA. You know what *you* looked like then, in your little velvet suit and floppy golden curls — a puppet child.

SASHA. I know I looked hideous! Was appallingly spoilt, (*Sharp smile straight at her.*) a very good example of what used to go on.

He moves past her, dodging her, getting to the other end of the carriage.

You know Polya, I still can't dress the way I want to.

POLYA (*mocking*). That's very serious.

SASHA. It is! I manage to hide the expensive gloves and scarf he makes me wear (*Moving*) and when he's not looking I wear this coat (*Indicates a grey coat.*) and then I look exactly the same as everybody else, almost *normal.* (*Very loud.*) Except for those shoes Polya — these terrible English shoes!

POLYA. What's the matter with them?

SASHA. What do you think, it's like they're on fire, they stand out a mile, everyone points at them.

He starts kicking the walls, smashing his feet against the corners, rubbing furiously.

I try to beat them down, I scuff them all the time, on the way to school every day.

POLYA (*laughs*). But they won't change!

SASHA. They're indestructible, they're so bloody strong, nothing I do makes any difference.

He sits, his legs splayed out, mauling the shoes, POLYA *laughs.*

When I have to go for a walk with Father — I keep well behind him.

Suddenly he's imitating his father in the middle of the carriage. POLYA *continues to laugh.*

He looks so ridiculous, strolling along, in that great coat, with a cane, in the shunting yards, among all this rolling stock here, freight being unloaded, and there he is saying good morning to everyone with a wave, like he's greeting farm labourers on his estate.

POLYA (*watching him*). What does it matter? If he thinks like that, I expect they enjoy it.

Pause.

SASHA (*slight smile, suddenly*). I tell people at school, I tell everyone he's an engine driver.

POLYA (*surprised*). You don't do that Sasha! You wouldn't.

SASHA. I do. (*Suddenly serious.*) Do you realise, Polya, he has never done a proper day's work in his life, not one, he's never even contemplated it!

POLYA. Of course he works — he has *his* work.

SASHA. What work? You don't mean *this*, I take it?

POLYA (*defiant*). Yes.

SASHA. The idea we have believed this for so long, haven't admitted what's happening, it's extraordinary — not even questioning it, just whispering about it when at last he's left that corner and gone out.

POLYA. *I* have never whispered about it.

SASHA. If I think of all the days since I was small, of creeping round the place in case I disturbed him . . . (*Loud*:) The truth is, and we've got to face it, Polya — (*Pointing at* NIKOLAI'*s corner*.) this is all useless, utterly useless — he's just a self-deluding old man.

POLYA (*shocked*). Sasha . . . (*Then sharply*.) He's not that old for a start!

SASHA (*incisively*). He contributes nothing, he receives money from the state for another purpose entirely, he has official duties which he ignores completely (*Loud*:) absolutely totally . . . That's the part I can't forgive; he takes the money which isn't his and then plays with his little pieces in a corner.

POLYA. Just plays, does he!

SASHA. He can't even fit these scraps together.

POLYA (*watching* SASHA'*s sharp, piercing stare*). I had no idea you were growing into such a nasty young . . .

SASHA. No, no, listen. (*Very incisive, trying to persuade her*.) Examine the facts Polya, please, for the first time in your life, this is very important. (*Moving, a commanding tone*.) It is not just that we have never seen him consult a single technical journal, or even use a single technical term when he's talking . . .

POLYA (*sharp*). So?

SASHA. We are being asked to believe that someone obsessed by eating off the right silver plate, using the right silver fish fork, is doing something of significance, is involved in technological progress!

POLYA (*defiant*). Yes!

SASHA (*continuing straight on*). It is a ludicrous proposition, obviously preposterous — it doesn't stand up to a moment's analysis. I mean he can't even boil a kettle. (*Loud*.) He can't even boil a bloody kettle, Polya.

POLYA. Nor could you till recently. (*Watching him*.)

SASHA. He told me what he was doing.

POLYA. He did?

SASHA. At the time you asked me I still remembered — but now I've long forgotten. He is a dilettante, Polya, a perfect instance of somebody refusing to change, placing his own needs above everybody else's — his individualism destroys others. I am *ashamed*, Polya, to be seen with him, to be associated with him in any way.

POLYA (*moving across*). You've got to stop this Sasha — you will stop it or I'll make you.

SASHA. Deny it if you can . . . you know you can't.

POLYA. Look at you. (*Catching hold of him, catching hold of his legs.*) Burrowing away to try to be as ordinary as possible.

SASHA (*incisive*). And what's more you still can't tear yourself away, can you — you can't bring yourself to leave despite having a room of your own now. (*Loud.*) You still come back for more — and he goes on exploiting you just the same.

POLYA (*loud, close*). Don't you start patronising me — give me lectures about what I should be doing. (*Very loud.*) It's my affair, don't you dare tell me what to do — if you ever talk to me like that again . . .

POLYA *seizes the fur coat SASHA does not wear anymore. The band plays outside.*

SASHA. I am just explaining the situation to you, Polya.

POLYA (*pinning him to the wall*). What a crude little animal you're turning out to be — afraid to stand out in a crowd are we?

She starts forcing him into the fur coat.

We'll see to that!

SASHA *tries to resist. They grapple by the window*, POLYA *winning. She gets the coat half on him, forcing his arms above his head.*

NIKOLAI *enters.* POLYA *has* SASHA *pinned against the wall.*

NIKOLAI *stands poised in the doorway in his fur coat, fur hat, and stick. He removes his hat, staring past them into the carriage.*

NIKOLAI. Is the place ready for me again? The washing is still out. (*He moves into the carriage.*) Bring me my tea, Polya, my tea and notes, my gloves need to dry . . .

NIKOLAI *hands* POLYA *his wet gloves, puts his stick on the table, and sits in the chair that is always reserved for him.* SASHA *leans against the wall watching* POLYA *run around.*

I have news. I have sent off through the emergency railway messenger service for a special delivery of my work — it is an unexpected bonus of this job, which is proving more and more useful . . .

SASHA *and* POLYA *exchange looks.* NIKOLAI *smiles. Waving a paper.*

I hear the special delivery should be arriving at any moment. (*He turns.*) Where is the tea?

POLYA (*sharp*). All right.

SASHA (*watching*). I have to write a dissertation, Papa, I was going to write about this city — but now I think I might write about an aspect of my family. (*Pause.*)

POLYA (*looking up, sharply, pause*). You wouldn't dare?

She suddenly moves over and starts bustling him out of the doors in his reluctant fur coat.

SASHA (*startled*). What are you doing?

POLYA. Sasha was just leaving, wasn't he? He's started to wear his old clothes again hasn't he?

She pushes a startled SASHA *out of the door, calling after him.*

Try taking that off — and you'll freeze to death before you get to school!

She pushes the door shut. The band is still rehearsing outside.

NIKOLAI. He is working hard, he is doing well at school.

POLYA. Who told you that?

NIKOLAI. He did of course. He wouldn't lie to me. (*Pause.*)

POLYA. He's very eager to fit in. (*Quiet.*) He'd do almost
anything for that.

NIKOLAI (*suddenly*). Eugenia! I saw her just now, hurrying
along the bridge. I must tell her how well she looks, years
younger, at least ten. (*Lightly.*) You must remind me to tell
her, Polya — but she has no need to work.

POLYA. She wants to.

NIKOLAI. She insists on doing a job! It is so utterly unnecessary
— Polya, why are you so slow today?

POLYA (*boiling kettle, making tea, loud*). Slow — I'm not being
slow!

NIKOLAI (*lightly*). You know at the moment there is only one
mechanism that I do not fully understand — (*He smiles.*) that
is the one that releases ideas, causes them to take shape.
(*Charming smile.*) It is becoming almost embarrassing how
many ideas I have at the moment, I am being bombarded by
them. Why now specially? (*Loud:*) Come on tea!

POLYA. Stop it. (*Loud:*) You don't yell for it anymore,
remember you wait for it now.

NIKOLAI. It seems I have little choice. Nevertheless hurry! I have
a lot to do. (*Slight pause.*) I have just completed my first task,
Polya. (*Calmly.*) I have made moving pictures talk. I have
solved the problem of amplification.

POLYA (*swinging round*). I thought so . . . I knew it! I guessed it
was something like that, when we found the camera under
here. (*Banging the drawer.*)

NIKOLAI. I am having some lenses made — the express order for
the northern railway.

POLYA (*excited*). Lenses! . . . Are they ready?

NIKOLAI (*smiling, calmly*). I have told them I need the
equipment urgently to record the erection of more telephone
poles for posterity. Even so, they've been extremely difficult

to obtain. When the lenses arrive I will be able to make some film and record the sound at the same time, it will be complete. (*Pause.*) And I am the first — I hope!

POLYA. You will have done it, Nikolai! (*Correcting herself:*) Nikolai Semenovitch. You will have done it!

NIKOLAI (*calmly*). The world has been working on two approaches, racing together, sound on phonograph records matched to keep pace with the image, and sound printed directly on film — I have achieved the second, which is undoubtedly the best and where the future lies.

POLYA (*moving excitedly*). So, when are they coming? The emergency delivery. When can we start?

NIKOLAI. Very soon. (*Calmly, simply:*) The effect naturally will be quite devastating. For better or worse it will revolutionise popular entertainment.

POLYA. Yes!

NIKOLAI. More importantly, it will alter communications — people will be able to talk to a huge audience out of the cinema screen, in a country of this size! Even quite complex ideas and information can now be spread across the continent. (*Pause, he smiles.*) I don't want to spend my time making grandiose claims, Polya — nothing could be more tiresome, nor more vulgar; but as you know, I *never* exaggerate.

POLYA. Once or twice, it has been known.

NIKOLAI. Absolutely wrong — it has never been known.

POLYA (*full of energy*). Where's it going to happen?

NIKOLAI. Here of course — you will all be photographed in this carriage. (*Lightly.*) The fact that the first sound film in the world will be recorded in the railway shunting yards outside Moscow . . . is not my fault.

POLYA (*loud*). You mean *us* on the screen — *me*! (*Suddenly, tone changing.*) I am not singing any of those appalling songs you made me sing — I don't sing well enough for that for a start. If I really have to sing — it's going to be a song of my choice. (*She moves.*) I might read a passage from a book.

(*Self-mocking smile.*) Whatever shows me off to my best advantage.

NIKOLAI. It will be a considerable shock to the outside world, that this is coming not out of California, or Paris, or even London, but out of here — coming out of the supposed darkness of this country.

POLYA (*moving backwards and forwards, excited, spirited smile*). Will our name be on it? Will mine? In the programme . . . "Polya, former domestic servant, second chambermaid, now a sorting clerk in the postal service, *recites.*" Me, flickering across the screen, thirty feet high!

She mimics flickering, jagged, movement across the screen. We suddenly see her as she would look on the screen.

All over the world. *My* voice squeaking out.

NIKOLAI. You may well become the best remembered postal clerk in Russia. A celebrity, someone people will want to meet. (*He smiles.*) I am confident nobody will realise it is a railway carriage — they will all assume it is a suite at the Hermitage if photographed correctly, so a semblance of dignity will be preserved, despite the farcical conditions in which history is being made.

POLYA *turns to face him.*

POLYA. It is exciting Nikolai Semenovitch!

NIKOLAI. Yes. Important as it is, and easily graspable for the general public though it is, it is comparatively trivial compared to what is to follow. (*He begins to move.*) There is much to do, I have made considerable progress on two other ideas, I need you for many more hours . . . to redraw my diagrams, you're much neater than I am, to prepare future model work (*He paces.*) — there is a limit I can use railway labour.

POLYA (*stops, her tone changes, firm*). No! I told you I can only fit you in after work, and I can't always go on as late as you want. (*Looking straight at him.*) I often won't be able to.

Pause. NIKOLAI *looks at her.*

NIKOLAI. You realise technological progress is being held up,

Polya, because you have to sort the grubby letters in the postal depot . . . major advances, may be halted just . . .

POLYA. I have explained to you many times why, and you still . . .

NIKOLAI (*cutting her off*). My God, Polya! — how can you be so wilful and stupid.

POLYA. Quite easily, I'm not going to work for you when I don't want to, only when I choose. (*Suddenly loud:*) Do you ever wonder why I stay, why I come back, time after time? No, you haven't, have you! Probably never crossed your mind.

Loud interrupted burst of band rehearsal outside, with sudden drumming, which ends as suddenly as it started.

(*Loudly, continuing as the band plays.*) And how I've never doubted your work. Never! Though I've been kept in almost total ignorance the whole time.

NIKOLAI. Why on earth should you have ever doubted it?

POLYA. Why!

NIKOLAI (*pacing too, they are both excited*). I can't believe we're wasting time with this! . . . I can't negotiate with you, Polya, there's too much to think about. (*He suddenly stops; his tone changes.*) I will continue your reading lessons, I will complete your studies, make sure you can read fluently.

POLYA (*furious, fiery*). I've been able to read for ages! Books this thick! You mean you haven't noticed that? (*Loud:*) No wonder you haven't mentioned it! (*Loud, moving:*) I could become a professor at a university and you still wouldn't see any difference.

NIKOLAI. I never thought you'd become so temperamental, Polya — so ridiculously pleased with yourself for some reason — and at such an inappropriate time!

POLYA. Me! I *am* — I'm being temperamental? (*She stops, loud:*) Why shouldn't I be anyway!

NIKOLAI *suddenly stops in the middle of the stage.*

NIKOLAI. I will do it without you! This time I will! Why should

I wait, for heaven's sake? (*Pause.*) I can't do it without you. There're certain things I cannot do. A few. (*Pause.*) How do you want me to ask you?

POLYA (*looking at him*). We'll do it together. (*Sharp:*) All right. But on my terms — (*Slight smile.*) — you're not paying me after all.

NIKOLAI. If I could explain to you what there is at stake — it is far more than talking film.

POLYA. Why don't you try telling me? Take the risk, I might even surprise you . . .

NIKOLAI. It is too technical for you.

He moves the width of the carriage; a solitary bell has started clanging in the distance.

(*Sharp, as he moves:*) I'm working on ways of advancing the use of wireless, making it far more accessible, ideas that have major implications for industry, and also, a by-product of the same idea, help the deaf . . .

Suddenly the band who have been making the noise outside the carriage break into the full, uninterrupted tune of the piece they have been rehearsing. It is a loud, stirring, but mournful funeral march. Behind the noise we can now hear many more bells clanging out.

Both NIKOLAI and POLYA turn towards the windows; a moment's silence as they are surprised by the noise. They are still.

My God what a noise. What's that for? Why can't they do that somewhere else?

POLYA (*by the window, loud*). They seem to have got it right at last. (*Calling out:*) About bloody time! (*She turns.*) It's a funeral march. Who do you think can have died?

Pause. The band plays the march. NIKOLAI *draws the blinds down on the windows of the carriage as the bells rasp out.*

NIKOLAI (*turning towards her*). Polya — we must to work now.

Blackout.

Scene Two

The music of the band and the rasping, tumultuous bells break into the noise of other trains moving round the carriage, clanking close; the sound of major movements, loud noises, then silence.

SASHA, *now back in his grey coat, enters the darkened carriage. In the middle of the carriage, standing where the bath was, is a large unopened packing case.*

SASHA *approaches it; he is unaware there is a figure sitting in the dark at the end of the carriage.*

SASHA (*starts, lets out a cry*). Comrade — I didn't see you, I didn't know we were expecting you.

VERKOFF *remains seated in the dark.*

VERKOFF. You weren't. (*Staring across.*) I must see your father at once, it is exceptionally urgent.

SASHA. My father's not here, as you can see.

VERKOFF. Where is he?

SASHA. I don't know, Comrade.

VERKOFF (*loud*). You have to know.

He gets up. His clothes are splashed with mud.

What happened to my letter? It must have arrived. (*Loud.*) It *has* arrived hasn't it?

SASHA. I am sure it has Comrade . . . my father tends to get a little behind with his correspondence — because he often throws letters away, but he will get better I assure you.

VERKOFF (*shouts*). You're not telling me he hasn't read it. (*Straight at him.*) Has he read it or not?

SASHA. I don't know, Comrade.

VERKOFF. You better find out.

A pale, blank stare from SASHA.

Who's been here?

SASHA. How do you mean?

VERKOFF. Has anybody visited here in the past weeks — been

poking around, looking at things, asking you questions?

SASHA. I don't think so, Comrade.

VERKOFF (*sharp*). Don't look away like that — look at me, come on tell me, what did they say? What did they want?

SASHA (*startled by his intensity*). Nothing . . . there was nobody here, Comrade.

VERKOFF. Don't you lie to me. (*Half mock-threatening, half-real:*) It can have terrifying consequences, do you understand me? (*Pause, slight smile.*) You *should* be afraid of me now.

SASHA. You know I'd tell you at once — if there was anything to tell.

VERKOFF. We shall see. (*He turns towards the packing case.*) What is this?

SASHA. That? (*Thinking quickly.*) Railway business, some supplies my father was just checking on. He's been waiting for them since just before the night Comrade Lenin died.

VERKOFF (*pushing the case*). Don't be ridiculous, this is not railway supplies. (*Loud:*) What did I just tell you?

He looks around for something to open it with, then picks up one of NIKOLAI's sticks and prises the top off.

SASHA. He talks more and more railway business, Comrade . . .

VERKOFF (*getting the top off, looking down inside, picking one of the lenses up gingerly*). So this is what he's been up to! (*Looking at the clutter of NIKOLAI's work things.*) I knew I was right about him — sometimes I wondered, I admit. But I knew I was right!

SASHA. Just a hobby, just a game of his.

VERKOFF. Shut up, be *quiet*. Stand over there where I can see you. Go on. (*Looking down at work things.*) I should have moved him earlier! (*Suddenly pointing, loud.*) Don't forget it was me who put you here. (*Loud:*) Never forget that!

SASHA. Yes, Comrade — I know.

VERKOFF (*moving, looking at everything*). When I first saw you all, together, first day in the country, standing in here, like relics from some Imperial Ball but looking pale and bloody terrified. Afraid to touch the sides in case you caught something.

SASHA (*hesitates, unsure of* VERKOFF's *tone*): . . . Yes, Comrade.

VERKOFF (*moving, loud*). I won't meet someone like your father again — the Jew so obsessed with his personal appearance, wrapping himself in the finest of everything, incapable of any form of political discussion, and then (*Looking down into the packing case.*) look at this! (*Loud.*) I *knew* I was correct about him!

SASHA (*suddenly*). I don't think you are correct about him, Comrade. My father is getting better. I know he's been neglectful, deviant, sometimes he's made me almost die of shame, but he will do his job, it takes a long time with him — to change him, to teach him.

VERKOFF (*loud*). You're going to teach him are you! (*Pause, he turns.*) You realise what I've done?

SASHA. Yes.

VERKOFF. What do you mean 'yes'? You don't have to give a blind sycophantic yelp to everything I say.

SASHA (*pauses*). Yes, Comrade.

VERKOFF (*suddenly exuberantly, lightly*). What I've done is incredibly important.

SASHA. I know.

VERKOFF. My job — the job I am doing — people could look at in years to come and see what looks like simple bureaucratic organisation, railways, telephone exchanges, drains, it might seem tedious, routine, mere clockwork — in truth the work was *fantastic.* You know why?

SASHA. Why, Comrade?

VERKOFF. Because I used my imagination — in a thousand different opportunities, small things, and major ones, I made some surprising decisions — every case was different, every case on its merits. (*He smiles.*) It was an inspired burst of planning.

SASHA. Yes I know — I've been forced to miss so much, having been away in the country so long, I'm only just catching up.

VERKOFF (*wry smile*). And who is going to remember an obscure official, tell me — one of the ministers of labour, of public works.

SASHA. They will, Comrade.

VERKOFF (*lightly*). People will always remember the obvious figures, naturally — everyone else gets bludgeoned onto the sidelines. Forgotten! (*Slight smile.*) But that is not the way things actually happen at the time. They will never realise what I did! That the department is spectacularly successful. Does it matter? It matters like hell to me at the moment. (*Pause. Suddenly sharp.*) And I can assure you I intend to keep it as long as possible. I'm certainly not done yet!

Pause. SASHA *stares at him.*

What a blank look that is. (*Pause.*) Your ignorance frightens me, boy. (*Suddenly, tone changing.*) Why am I here anyway? This is just one small part of my department, one tiny corner, why am I wasting my time with a child?

SASHA. Yes, Comrade.

VERKOFF *stares at the pale face of the teenage boy.*

VERKOFF. You're as bad as them do you know that — you have to be told what you ought to think, have to be absolutely sure what the correct thing to say is before you dare open your mouth.

SASHA *stares at him.*

The physical effort required to talk to people who only deal in certainties, you have no idea! It's so bloody tiring! (*Pulling him closer.*) Come here — so who was it that came here, come on, tell me, I know somebody was.

SASHA. No. They haven't, I promise you.

VERKOFF (*slight smile*). Just checking, I'm not at all sure I believe you. (*Pause, staring at the boy.*) The furniture has suddenly been changed in my office.

SASHA. Has it, Comrade — is it an improvement?

VERKOFF (*shrewd look*). We shall see . . . now listen to me carefully, so there is no possibility of error, I'm instructing you to leave the country — and this instruction has to be obeyed in the next few days!

SASHA (*stunned*). Leave the country? What do you mean in the next few days?

VERKOFF. That's what you have to do.

He scrawls a one-line note on a scrap of paper.

SASHA. Has papa been that negligent? I told you he will get better — he will do his duties . . .

VERKOFF (*lightly*). I will put it very simply so it can be intelligible even to you — it is a small matter of life and death.

SASHA. Life and death?

VERKOFF. For all of you.

SASHA. All of us?

VERKOFF. Those are my orders to you. And find that letter! (*He moves.*) If you ever get to the border that letter might make it a great deal easier for you to leave. (*Pause.*) Or it might not.

SASHA (*worried*). That isn't very clear, Comrade, if I may say so . . .

VERKOFF. I must go! I have so many people to see. (*Suddenly looking down at his clothes, at the door.*) Good God, I'm covered in mud, I never noticed, why didn't you tell me? Didn't you see? (*Sharp smile.*) Because it's a form of uniform you never noticed! (*As he goes:*) You know what you have to do, you have to try and leave.

He goes.

SASHA (*moving over to the door, calling after him*). But he won't go — he won't go until he's finished his work, Comrade. (*Pause, anger rising.*) Don't you understand, he won't leave until he's finished his crazy work — he's under the impression he's doing something important. (*Loud shouts, close by the door.*) What am *I* meant to do — he won't listen to me. He can't be made to stop don't you realise? He won't stop his 'work' don't you see! (*Turning back into the carriage.*) How can I do anything? . . .

He breaks off, staring at the box in the middle of the carriage. He lifts off the top prised open by VERKOFF, *and lets it drop onto the floor.*

I think whatever these are . . .

He dips his hands in and lifts up a glass lens wrapped in straw, so the glass catches the light, flashes out brightly.

Whatever they happen to be — they will have to go.

He drops the lens back onto the others in the box, making a clanking noise.

Can I do it? (*Staring into the box.*) It has to be good enough to *stop* him.

He picks up a hammer and a long knife from among the equipment lying in his father's corner; he moves back to the box; he lifts one of the lenses again and runs the top of the knife down it, scratching its surface. Then he knocks the lens with a clean, sharp hit from the hammer. It splits in two.

Very pale, he stands with the hammer and a long metal bar taken from the side, staring down into the box. He chooses to do it with the hammer. Suddenly he swings it again and again into the box. The hammer goes up above his head, coming down with startling ferocity with each blow.

Must destroy it so he can't start up again — no *chance* of him trying to start again. It mustn't mean we have to stay even longer. (*Loud:*) Has to go!

A ferocious burst of destruction as he pummels the contents of the box.

SASHA *hears the sound of them approaching,* POLYA's *voice and laughter.*

(*Looking around him very fast.*) Better do something else . . .

SASHA *runs round the length of the carriage upturning furniture, turning drawers out, tearing sheets down the middle with the long knife, slashing some of the chairs, the beds. Just before* POLYA *enters he begins to try to scratch some graffiti – a slogan on the ornamental panelling – but drops the knife and kicks it under the bunk, as* POLYA *reaches the door. He leans against the wall very still, looking pale.* POLYA *enters, stares at the destruction.*

POLYA (*shocked, quiet*). Sasha – what on earth has happened?

SASHA *stares from the far end of the carriage.*

SASHA. There's been an attack – some people got in . . . and they've done this –

POLYA *moves slowly into the carriage.*

POLYA. Who were they? (*Pause.*) I mean they've torn the place apart, Sasha.

SASHA. I've just come back . . . I just found it, now.

POLYA (*suddenly looking at him, moving close to him*). Are you all right – not hurt, Sasha, love? (*Touching him.*) They didn't do anything to you, didn't attack you . . .

SASHA (*as she touches his face*). I just missed them . . .

POLYA. No, nothing . . .

She withdraws, disappointed at herself for showing such warm feelings towards him.

You were very lucky.

She looks across the carriage.

Who would have wanted to attack here?

SASHA. He may have enemies, he's a target now . . . (*Suddenly:*) The Commissar of Labour came – just now – he saw it, he couldn't stay, he left this note, Polya.

POLYA (*looks down at the shattered glass and equipment in the box*). Oh my God not here, too.

She picks up a broken lens.

SASHA. No point doing that — it won't work. You can't do anything.

POLYA (*looking very pale, suddenly moving*). Your father — what will he do? He's just coming, he's waited months for these. It's so *important*. He could kill people for this. (*Quiet:*) So could I. (*Sharp:*) Why did they come just now, how did they *know* this was here? (*Moving.*) What can we do to lessen . . .

NIKOLAI *enters with* EUGENIA. *He immediately stops in the door, stock still.*

NIKOLAI. What have you two been doing?

EUGENIA (*staring around her*). Oh no, Sasha. (*Sharp:*) Who's done this?

POLYA. Nikolai Semenovitch prepare yourself . . . There's been an attack as you can see, and . . . (*She stops.*)

SASHA (*quiet*). There's also a note from the Commissar of Labour telling us to leave.

He holds it out and EUGENIA *takes it.*

Silence.

NIKOLAI (*standirg in the doorway pointing at the packing case with his stick, calmly*). Are they all broken?

POLYA. Yes, they're broken.

NIKOLAI (*calmly*). Not just the lenses. All of it?

POLYA. All of it.

Pause.

NIKOLAI (*voice very precise, deadly calm*). I don't think that will prove too much of a problem.

Slight pause.

All of them smashed, all broken — it doesn't present too much of a problem, no . . .

Pause, voice rising, suddenly dangerous.

It just means I will not be able to finish my work.

He is very still, but the rage is beginning to pass through his body.

Those who did this have to be found — they will have to be dealt with in the only way that is fitting . . .

Pause. They all stare at him.

They will have to be hunted down wherever they have chosen to hide themselves and be destroyed.

EUGENIA (*moving, not daring to go too close to him*).
Nikolai . . . I know . . . what's happened is a terrible shock, (*Holding* VERKOFF's *note.*) but there's also this.

NIKOLAI (*cutting her off, suddenly the shout comes out*). My God, why do people do such things — have this desire to smash and tear up anything they don't understand — this compulsion to stamp all over it. I hope they realise I am capable of just as much and *more*. I can be as violent as they are and more effective. They will be found. They will be made to face what they have done, they've tried to extinguish — four years' work — waste all the effort that has been going on in here. Kill it.

POLYA. Maybe we can . . . (*Looking at the broken pieces.*)

NIKOLAI. I can assure you — they will not succeed. I will not let them succeed.

Pause.

EUGENIA. My love, I'm not sure we can afford to ignore this note from the Commissar of Labour, instructing us to leave the country; he says he sent us a letter . . .

NIKOLAI *takes the note, but continues to pace. Pause.*

NIKOLAI. I will do it still. That is both a promise and a warning and nothing can stop that now.

Pause. A quick glance at the note.

And there is no question of me fleeing this country. (*At the door*.) Whoever did this didn't realise one thing, I can still manage to do it.

He goes. Both women move back and forth across the carriage automatically, picking up the shattered pieces, trying to patch the torn interior of the carriage together.

EUGENIA. Nikolai . . . (*Staring at the mess.*) I knew something from the outside would come bursting in here one day, all the different things moving round us in this shunting yard. I'm almost surprised it's nothing worse.

POLYA (*staring at the broken equipment*). It's bad enough. But he will find a way. Whoever tried to stop him, won't.

SASHA *stares from the wall.*

EUGENIA (*loud, suddenly*). Polya — this could just be a taste of what is to come — do we try to stay or do we leave?

POLYA. I don't know.

EUGENIA. Even if we get to the border we might have to stay there for weeks and if anything went *wrong* there . . . (*Her voice falls off.*) No second chances. (*Turns, determined.*) We have to find that letter from the Minister of Labour before there are any official changes, we have to use it . . . perhaps we could use a health reason. (*She is moving up and down.*) If we decide to leave — I heard people were doing that — (*Pause.*) we could say something like mine or Sasha's health is unlikely to stand up to another winter . . .

POLYA (*smiles*). It's only spring now.

EUGENIA (*moving*). I know!

POLYA. It might work . . .

EUGENIA. Nikolai would never agree of course.

POLYA. I could use your travel permits, travel with you, some of the way to the border, and then move down south, get away from the trouble here, find a new job!

EUGENIA (*looking up*). You might be better off leaving at once — the danger may be getting contagious, being with us.

Slight pause.

POLYA. Not yet.

EUGENIA. I don't know, Polya, I would never forgive myself if something happened to you because of us.

POLYA (*turning*). It will be fine . . .

EUGENIA. Maybe Nikolai, to finish his work, can get supplies from abroad. I know so little about it.

POLYA. You've got to *tell* him, Eugenia, whatever you decide . . . it's your future too.

EUGENIA (*turning, unsure*). It may not matter — our extraordinary luck will probably hold.

SASHA (*watching them*). Polya should stay with us as long as possible.

POLYA. You want that now, do you? (*Pause.*) What for? Protection?

SASHA. Advice . . . We'll need your advice.

POLYA (*advancing towards him*). Really? The problem is I don't like you very much at the moment, Sasha. Remember?

SASHA. That doesn't matter now.

POLYA (*staring at him, then touching his hair*). Speak for yourself.

Blackout.

Scene Three

The carriage at the border — the sound of movement, of trains passing very close, loud braking noises, the wrenching of metal, the feeling of large important movements of people, of machines, in the night. Voices calling sporadically in the distance, phones ringing and stopping and ringing again, a sense of contained chaos. The noise punctuated by bouts of silence.

The sounds continue to erupt again from time to time, close to them, brushing right up to them, near the window.

SASHA, EUGENIA, POLYA and NIKOLAI all together in the carriage. It is night, the packing cases have been pushed back into a corner — the pigskin luggage is splayed all over the carriage half open, but most of their possessions are still around the carriage. EUGENIA is moving around with their clothes, POLYA lifts the blind of one of the windows to stare out, a passing light stabs through at them and is gone. Their mood is tense but excited, NIKOLAI sits calmly in the middle of them all.

POLYA pulls the blind right up.

EUGENIA. What can you see, Polya?

POLYA. Just an old woman holding a fluffy dog out of another train window so it can pee.

SASHA (*by the other window*). Just blackness here; there's that ringing all the time — I can't see from where. (*Jumping up by the window, climbing up*.) I can just see the corner of something, a shape. (*Excited smile.*) As usual it's just out of sight — another hundred yards and we'd have a much better view!

Incessant ringing in the distance.

POLYA. It's one of the telephones ringing in the Guard posts by the other platforms — nobody ever seems to answer it.

EUGENIA. We've got here anyway — I never thought we'd do it, reach the border. (*She turns.*) We probably shouldn't have given our passes to those young soldiers — we should have kept them with us, not given them too long a look.

POLYA. They were friendly enough.

NIKOLAI (*lightly*). They will be no problem, they have seen I am with you. They are just clearing a path so they can move us across the border. The next train that has been approved to go through — we will be joined up to that one.

POLYA (*sharp smile*). You've always hated to queue anyway! (*She moves.*) There're so many trains here, going back in all directions, I'm spoiled for choice, which one I take to the south.

EUGENIA (*quietly*). I keep thinking you ought to have got off earlier, Polya . . .

NIKOLAI. We will be allowed to stay in this until they turn it round across the border. (*Indicates the carriage.*) The last we'll see of this won't be until we're in Poland, (*Quiet:*) where we will drink the champagne, (*Indicates the champagne.*) one of the few bottles left. (*Pause.*) When I return in a few weeks I will of course reclaim the carriage.

EUGENIA (*moving*). You will remember, Nikolai, you're not going to talk about your work to them — or even much about your job for the government. The less we say the better — we're not going to tell the *whole* truth.

NIKOLAI (*calm*). I remember, yes.

EUGENIA. And we still haven't found that letter from the Minister of Labour.

POLYA (*sharp, by the window, the noise close to them*). Did you see they were letting no one stay on the platform — people sitting and sleeping on the bank along the line for about three miles.

EUGENIA. And they seemed to have dropped their belongings everywhere, all over the rails, a lot of people do it on purpose I think — getting rid of valuables they think they better not risk.

POLYA (*climbing up by the window, straining to see*). Yes, you can just see back there, on that huge pile of coal by the line. It's shining with all the things they've thrown out of the windows, people's silver . . .

EUGENIA. Thank God we got rid of ours, and the firearms, too.

NIKOLAI *is sitting calmly in the middle.*

POLYA (*to* SASHA). Are you going to do well — do what you have to do?

SASHA. I think so.

EUGENIA (*nervous smile*). Does he look pale enough, do you think?

POLYA. His cheeks are blooming, of course — (*To* SASHA:) Try to make you look ill and you seem to get healthier by the minute, never seen you look so well! Come on, let's hear you cough, harder, *cough*.

SASHA. I am coughing!

NIKOLAI (*quiet*). That won't be necessary.

POLYA (*touching* SASHA). I haven't liked you for many months you know, not until the last few days.

SASHA. Polya — there's something I did, I'll have to tell you one day.

The door opens, GUARD 1 *and* GUARD 2 *enter.*

They are dressed in heavy coats, new uniforms, very bulky in the confined space. They look totally different, almost unrecognisable, older, more haggard. The small, stocky GUARD 2 *much less exuberant, much more deferential to the younger* GUARD 1, *who is more efficient, confident, authoritative. They show no sign of recognising* NIKOLAI, *their manner brisk from having had to process so many people.*

GUARD 1 (*looking at his clipboard, then at the passengers grouped at one end of the carriage*). These your papers here ... Nikolai Pesiakoff ...

NIKOLAI. Yes ...

For the first time his manner is unsure, not certain how to dissemble.

As you can see they are clear, everything is self-explanatory, there is no problem.

GUARD 1 (*looking down at the papers*). Destination London, via

Berlin . . . that certainly is clear enough. Three travel permits.

EUGENIA (*sharp*). Yes!

GUARD 1 (*looks up at* POLYA). What are you doing here?

POLYA. I'm not staying with them. I'm just a friend, I am here to change trains.

NIKOLAI (*suddenly looking straight at the* GUARDS). What are your names?

GUARD 1. Our names? That need not concern you. (*Looking at him.*) Allow us to ask the questions.

NIKOLAI. I am almost certain, I don't think I'm wrong, we have met before. At another station, much smaller than this one, somewhere along that vast bleak stretch of the northern railway, which at one time I had to move up and down.

GUARD 1 (*calmly*). I can assure you we have never met before. (*Moving with the papers.*) Now what are your reasons for wishing to travel outside the country, comrade?

EUGENIA. The reasons are on our papers. It's all set down, we told the other guards.

GUARD 1 (*calmly*). I know what your papers say — but I want to hear your version. (*Staring at them.*) It's our normal procedure.

NIKOLAI. You want me to tell you? (*Pause.*) The reasons we are leaving, I mean we're travelling . . . I am escorting my family out of the country because . . . (*He stops.*) we have obtained permission because . . . (*He falters, finding it difficult to lie.*) because my son's health is . . . because when, if the winter is, when the winter . . . (*He stops.*)

EUGENIA. My husband has had a long journey, please remember.

NIKOLAI. Because my son must . . .

SASHA. Papa, I will tell them.

NIKOLAI. No! (*Pause.*) I am not going to go on with this, it is an unbelievable excuse, I am not going to lie to you, I have not had enough practice for one thing and do it poorly, and it insults your intelligence.

He looks straight at the GUARDS.

I am Nikolai Pesiakoff. I am taking my family across the
border and then I will be returning almost immediately — in
time we will all return I assure you. I am appointed the
Telephone Examiner of the northern district by Commissar
of Labour Alexei Verkoff — this carriage has been made
available for my use.

Pause. They are all watching him.

More importantly I have some vital work to complete which
should prove of some use. (*Pause.*) I will be ordering some new
components and equipment from abroad and returning, so you
see you have merely to rubber stamp our permits. It is all a
formality. Moreover, I am certain you must remember this
now, I recommended you two for promotion when we
stumbled across each other, in exchange for some help you
gave me in finding some equipment for my work. (*He smiles.*)
It happens to be one of the few official letters I ever wrote.
You will remember this all now taking place I am sure, in the
northern district — (*He smiles straight at them.*) so although it
appears to be a coincidence that we find each other, it is in
fact only a partial one.

Silence. The GUARDS *are watching him.*

GUARD 1. I have been very patient . . .

GUARD 2. You are trying to tell us you were the Telephone
Surveyor of the Northern Railway.

NIKOLAI. Of course.

GUARD 2 (*loud*). That is not true.

GUARD 1 (*moving around the carriage, looking at everything,
manner methodical, but sharp*). It is certainly not true. I did
indeed meet him. I can't remember it all, it was some time ago
and a great deal has happened since then, but one thing I know
for certain, he could have been nothing like you.

GUARD 2. I remember him a bit, he arrived out of the night, and
he was nothing like you, (*Sharp, party manner.*) a very
conscientious official. *Punctillious.*

NIKOLAI (*calmly*). That person was I — it seems odd that it is you who look different not me, but I recognise you. (*Lightly.*) I recommended you for a position of increased responsibility. It appears to have worked almost too well.

GUARD 2 (*loud*). You're not him, all right? No influence was used in getting us where we are, either, I can tell you.

He begins a search of the carriage.

EUGENIA (*sharp*). What's he doing?

NIKOLAI. Who do you think I am then? How else could I possibly be in this — (*Indicating the carriage.*) — and got it joined to a train coming to the border?

GUARD 1 (*very incisive; suddenly we see how overworked and tense he is*). My God — don't waste my time, we have people arriving here in all sorts of ways, all forms of transport, having bribed, cajoled, sometimes killed, to get here — even just to get themselves a compartment to themselves. (*As GUARD 2 searches.*) And we have to deal with them all. People being arrogant or worse, obsequious, people trying to squeeze through holes that haven't been plugged, before it's too late. Pushing, refusing to wait, shouting out and complaining all night, grabbing hold of your arm, poking you in the face with their sticks.

GUARD 2. Last night somebody shouted at me — what I thought was a frail old man — he screamed, 'I don't expect you've ever seen a golf club before, you ignorant fool.' He then lifted it above his head and smashed it through the air at me.

He demonstrates, then turning to EUGENIA, hands her some letters he's uncovered.

Are these yours?

EUGENIA (*grabbing them*). Yes.

GUARD 1 (*looking at NIKOLAI*). And the lies we have to deal with too, some very clumsy, so obvious, but some very elaborate, people producing whole new histories for themselves, whole new lives they say they've led, views they've never held, reasons why they *have* to travel.

GUARD 2. Some of them don't pretend at all but *demand* to be let out at *once*.

GUARD 1 (*quiet, strong*). So many of them desperate to leave the land of their birth − the country is disgorging people at the moment, the waste that didn't leave before is finally leaving now. Some of it can be allowed to drain out, many others have to stay because of what they've done. (*He moves.*) We have lists, and we can't afford to make mistakes.

A phone rings in the background.

That telephone never ever stops ringing with news, instructions. Of all the teams working here, we are the team being held responsible.

GUARD 2. I have never worked so hard in my entire life!

NIKOLAI (*calm*). You will remember me.

GUARD 2 *suddenly moves across the carriage, having found a package in a silk bag.*

GUARD 2. Look at this! (*Handing it to* GUARD 1.)

GUARD 1 (*holds the silk bag*). Can you explain these, comrade?

NIKOLAI (*calmly*). They are diamonds.

EUGENIA (*surprised by this find, but immediately recovering*). We were *allowed* to take some diamonds out, family possessions, we . . .

GUARD 1. Nobody is allowed to take such things as diamonds out of the country. (*Staring at them.*) Why weren't they on your form? Among your papers?

EUGENIA (*sharp*). There's so much to write down, somehow they got left out.

GUARD 1. You left out diamonds?

POLYA. They would have been better hidden if we'd intended to hide them, wouldn't they?

NIKOLAI (*calmly*). They were not hidden in any way, I would never allow that.

GUARD 1 (*staring at them*). None of you must now leave this carriage, for any reason. You will remain here. (*Pause.*) If you are right and you sought permission, which was granted, this will be the first time this has happened. If you're wrong — the consequences could be grave. (*Moving to exit.*) We will have to make a telephone call. We will see.

GUARD 1 *and* GUARD 2 *exit.*

EUGENIA (*loud*). Why did you keep those, Nikolai — why on earth did you bring the diamonds with us? (*She looks at him.*) I thought we had got rid of everything.

NIKOLAI. I wanted you to have security abroad when I had to leave you, some source of income. (*Pause.*) Perhaps you should have been wearing them — we should have been even more straightfoward.

EUGENIA. Whatever the reason, that wasn't wise, Nikolai . . . it could be very serious.

NIKOLAI. Don't worry — at the worst they will attempt to confiscate them — but I will get them back.

EUGENIA *starts looking through the unopened letters the* GUARD *found.*

He couldn't remember me, the guard. He was not lying, I don't blame him, he is quite busy. He was thinking how I must have looked in retrospect — slightly nervous of the truth, so he simply altered it. He'll remember.

EUGENIA (*looking up sharply*). This is *the* letter Nikolai, the one that was thrown away so effectively, the Minister of Labour's letter.

POLYA. It's found.

NIKOLAI. What does he say? Is it of any use to us?

EUGENIA (*staring down first page of letter, eager*). He says . . . he says . . . my God!

POLYA. What?

EUGENIA (*reads*). 'When you first came into my office with all those ideas — this ludicrous even grotesque figure, I had to restrain my clerks from tearing you to pieces — but your *ideas*, your papers you submitted? I didn't understand them — but they were extraordinary'.

SASHA (*surprised*). Extraordinary?

EUGENIA (*carrying straight on*). 'Despite the fact that they were written on note paper from the Ritz Hotel in Paris!

NIKOLAI *is impassive.*

'You certainly didn't look a likely inventor of anything — could such modern notions which would actually work be churning around in such a person?'

Pause.

'The answer was *yes* . . . maybe, perhaps. The trouble was if I gave you space to work in Moscow people would literally probably strangle you inside a week.'

NIKOLAI. Proceed.

EUGENIA (*excited*). I can't believe this. (*She reads.*) 'I had an inspiration! One of the many I had at the time — I WILL MAKE HIM TELEPHONE EXAMINER BEFORE THERE IS ANY REAL NEED FOR ONE.'

POLYA. What! (*Reading over her shoulder.*) 'I will give him a place of his own, a Government appointment that will protect him, access to labour and funds if he chooses to use them.'

EUGENIA. 'I knew you wouldn't do a stroke of Railway work — as it is I received some delightful lies from your wife.' (EUGENIA *breaks off.*) He might have told me, mightn't he! (*She returns to letter.*) 'Some of which are on my wall staring at me now.'

POLYA. Yes, yes, why didn't he let *us* know?

SASHA *suddenly grabs the second page of letter and starts to read from the top of the page.*

SASHA. 'I knew if you succeeded, Nikolai, you would break every door down in Moscow to show people — if you failed, if you were a fraud, I could just write it off as Railway expense.' (*Reading fast, agitated, realising his own grave mistake.*) 'And Nikolai, I knew if I told you the *truth* you wouldn't stand it

for a moment and would be camping on a doorstep, refusing
to go, telling my staff they weren't dressed properly, that they
were all ignorant peasants! *So, you got put in the carriage —
and it is just beginning, I hope, to bear some sort of fruit'.*
(*To himself.*) Oh! 'I have to break off in a hurry, I have other
urgent letters to write.'

NIKOLAI (*loud.*) Give me that letter!

SASHA (*moving away*). Oh my god, what have I done . . .? Polya,
you don't know what I've done. I've been so stupid, didn't see
anything. I have done something terrible, truly terrible.

POLYA (*concerned*). What's the matter with you?

NIKOLAI (*commanding*). Sasha, quiet . . . (*Silence. He takes the
letter. Calmly:*) The idiot — why didn't he explain this to me,
he treated me like a child. I failed to understand the use of
'ludicrous' and 'grotesque' . . . and he seems almost as vain as I
am. (*Pause.*) Nevertheless he could have done worse — it is true
he could have done much worse.

EUGENIA (*with feeling*). Yes.

NIKOLAI. There was a mind at work there, an intelligence.
(*Slight smile.*) He enjoyed my contradictions. (*Lightly.*) It
might even be a document of historical interest — all the more
reason to complete the task.

POLYA (*tense smile*). And you can still do it with *me*, which is
important, still got the chance. (*Moving, febrile, by the
window.*) Find some new equipment round here and as the
first talking film, you can have me singing at the border.
Wailing out of a window!

NIKOLAI. Yes.

The sound of movement outside.

POLYA. You can use some of the people outside, the people
queuing, and the guards, you can have them all telling their
stories, record the faces and shouts from the border . . .

NIKOLAI (*slight smile*). Finding the equipment here, Polya, is
slightly unlikely, but this — (*Holding the Minister of Labour's
letter.*) — this is a splendid find, we have no problem now. We

just give them the letter — it shows who I am — it is a proof of everything.

EUGENIA. I don't think that would be wise. (*She takes the letter.*)

NIKOLAI. Why, how can it not be?

EUGENIA. We don't know where he is now — what has happened to him. Until we know that, I'm not sure anyone should read it. (*Glancing down at the letter.*) He's written this in such a hurry, so urgently, it's stained all over with ink, and sweat.

The door opens suddenly. GUARD 2 *enters.*

NIKOLAI. You have brought our papers now I hope.

GUARD 2 (*pointing straight at* POLYA). Right, she has to leave, come on get your things and *out.*

POLYA. Me? (*Startled pause.*) Why now?

GUARD 2. You don't get to ask questions, you do as you're told. You've got to leave, so you get up, take a few things, and you get out of here!

POLYA. I will leave how I like, in my own time.

GUARD 2 (*shouts*). Don't play around with me — I haven't slept for three nights, you realise, and it's getting worse all the time, it never ever stops —

Phones and noise in the background.

So don't you try arguing. (EUGENIA *lifts her head.*) The rest of you keep quiet!

POLYA (*moving deliberately over to* SASHA). Sasha, despite everything — (*Gives him a kiss, slightly formal.*) — I think I might even miss you.

Then turning, instinctively reverting to her former role for a second, checking clothes.

You know where all your winter clothes are — in which suitcase, where the thick socks are?

SASHA (*moving after her*). Polya, you're not still angry with me? (*Loud.*) You're not to be. I wanted so much to belong, that's all — wanted to be part of things, what was happening . . .

POLYA (*looking at him again*). Yes, I know.

SASHA (*quiet*). . . . and all the time it seems I was nearer to it than I thought, Papa's work . . .

GUARD 2. I told you to get a move on . . .

SASHA. One day I'll tell you what I did . . . when things are easier I'll . . .

POLYA (*staring at him*). When that happens, I'll want to hear it.

SASHA. I destroyed something, Polya.

POLYA (*touching him*). Worry about things in the past later, you've got to be strong now, Sasha.

GUARD 2 (*suddenly turning to* NIKOLAI). Right, now you, take that coat off and give it to me.

Pause.

NIKOLAI. For any particular reason?

GUARD 2. Just do as I say — everything will be much simplier if you do that.

NIKOLAI (*calmly, taking the great coat off*). Do I get a receipt?

EUGENIA. What are you doing? What's happening?

GUARD 2 (*to* NIKOLAI). Now the jacket, and the shirt, go on give them to me. (*To* EUGENIA:) Your husband is shortly going to be removed from this carriage, he will be charged tonight, and taken away from here for sentence.

POLYA (*loud*). Why?

EUGENIA. Where's the trial? Where's he going?

GUARD 2 (*cutting her off*). You and the child are forbidden to stay, you continue out of the country tonight. (*Sharp.*) You understand? (*To* NIKOLAI:) Now take your shoes. (*Pointing at his polished feet.*) Fine shoes there, take them off, and your socks, off! (*As* NIKOLAI *hesitates:*) I don't want to hurt anybody, but there's an allocated time for each person, so just do it.

NIKOLAI. I have no intention of running away.

> NIKOLAI *obeys their instructions. Without his magnificent coat, gloves, hat, the jacket of his suit, his shirt, he is left in his vest and trousers, barefoot, looking frail and vulnerable, suddenly older, whiter; but he is sitting very straight, in the middle of the carriage.*

POLYA (*watching* NIKOLAI *undress*). You don't have to do that to him.

GUARD 2 (*looking at* POLYA *and her papers*). Why on earth did you bother staying with this lot anyway? (*Glancing at them.*) Cleaning up after them, running around . . . why?

POLYA (*facing him*). So *you're* allowed to ask questions and I'm not.

EUGENIA (*warning*). Polya . . .

GUARD 2 (*sharp*). Why?

POLYA. I did it for my own reasons, because *I* wanted to. Because I was doing something important here with him — yes, with *him*.

> *Indicating* NIKOLAI, GUARD 2 *looks disbelieving.*

One way and another a lot of me had gone into it, it was my work as well as his. (*With feeling:*) And I really *did* want to see it through more than *you* can imagine. And we've just reached a point as it happens when . . .

> *A phone rings in the distance, but louder.*

GUARD 2. There's that phone! Come on, get ready now! (*Holds the rolls of fur that is the coat, and looking at him*). That's more like it.

NIKOLAI (*calmly to the women*). It is all right, this is only very temporary.

GUARD 2. Everything out of the pockets, empty the pockets.

> *He shouts through the window at the ringing phone.*

Stop that ringing for God's sake, answer the bloody thing.

POLYA (*loud, powerful*). He'll die the death of cold — I haven't spent all this time with him — to see him wiped out by pneumonia. (*She turns.*) What harm has he done, what harm could he possibly do?

EUGENIA (*warning*). Polya . . .

GUARD 2. We're finding out a lot more about him now — information is still coming through from Moscow. (*To POLYA:*) Now have you got what you want — otherwise you will leave with nothing. (*He looks around the carriage.*)

POLYA (*loud*). And stop ferreting around — there is nothing else to find.

NIKOLAI. Polya . . . there is no need for that.

POLYA (*facing him*). I've known each of these people for years — it is not possible to say goodbye in a few seconds and I won't . . .

GUARD 2 (*briskly, not unpleasantly*). You get extremely used to seeing people do it, all ages, all kinds of relationships, it's much simpler this way I can assure you.

POLYA (*to* NIKOLAI). They will realise they are making a mistake.

NIKOLAI. Naturally, I will be returning ready to resume very soon Polya. (*To the* GUARD:) Some heating here would now be appreciated.

GUARD 2. No chance, this is no longer a hotel. (*Really tense.*) Don't give me any more trouble, all right?

POLYA *goes up to* EUGENIA.

POLYA. Eugenia . . .

EUGENIA (*touching her*). I don't know how I will live without seeing you.

POLYA. You'll manage — you know where everything is.

EUGENIA. I didn't mean that. (*Worried.*) You know I didn't mean about domestic things, Polya, I . . .

GUARD 2 (*breaking in, pulling* POLYA *by her arm*). Come on, that's enough.

POLYA (*back to* EUGENIA). Of course I . . . (*Fighting the*

GUARD.) Stop it, stop that.

The GUARD *grabs at her, short sharp grabs at her. She fights him off, till he's really got her. Suddenly she's dragged out of the carriage very forcibly and is gone.*

EUGENIA. She's left and I didn't make myself clear what I meant. (*She moves. Loud.*) She's gone and she thought I was talking about domestic work.

POLYA *appears framed in one of the windows, staring back at them, looking startled, pale, as there is the sound of the door being fastened from the outside. Then she is forcibly moved away, suddenly, looking very frightened, telephones ringing in the distance.*

NIKOLAI. Polya . . .

EUGENIA. Why are they being so rough with her? They'll let her get her train, won't they?

NIKOLAI. Yes, they will.

EUGENIA (*to* NIKOLAI). What are they going to do, how will they treat *you*?

NIKOLAI. Sasha, don't look so frightened.

SASHA (*very quiet*). No, Papa . . .

NIKOLAI. There will be no further problems — they seem to be being terrified by messages down the telephone, but they won't seriously attempt to detain me. (*Pause.*) My feet are cold, that's all. (*Sitting in his vest, carrying on as if nothing had happened.*) It may be difficult, though, for me to return here to Russia — for some time.

Pause.

(*Acidly:*) What a destination! What a fate. To end up in England!

EUGENIA. I thought that's what you always wished for, above all.

NIKOLAI (*astonished*). Always wished for! (*Pause.*) The idea horrifies me. (*Self-mocking smile.*) When I went there I had an utterly miserable time, grey and utterly sodden. (*He looks round the carriage.*) They're terribly slow the English, you have to explain everything so many times, they think in such a literal way. It is all so rigid there, they treat their servants appallingly. (*Incisive*:) There is no energy of ideas, they instinctively distrust nearly all ideas on sight, and they like you to apologise for having thought of them. They thought I was mad and exceedingly arrogant, they backed away from me when I came into the room, always looked at their feet. They have a terror of everything foreign. (*Lightly*:) They will not believe in me, this 'grotesque' did not and will not go down well. (*Slight smile.*) Also, and even more important, the coffee is disgusting, undrinkable.

EUGENIA. You never told me — you never told me that's what happened.

The sound of movement around them.

NIKOLAI. No, and we haven't got the money to reach America. (*Slight smile.*) Might be worse of course. (*Tone changing*:) It is interesting isn't it, being on the edge of the country. Nothing I have ever read or been told in my life has prepared me for this shock, the sheer physical sensation when one is faced with leaving one's native land permanently — like you are being pulled away from a magnetic field and that everything will then stop. It will have been severed. (*Calm.*) An illogical fear maybe but my God it's strong. As far as I'm aware mere fame has never been what drove me on in my work. I wanted to do it here. Leaving suddenly feels distinctly unnatural and dangerous.

EUGENIA. I know, I can feel it. I'm not sure that's all that's going to happen, Nikolai. (*She puts a blanket around him.*)

NIKOLAI. If they were going to shoot me — they would have probably done it already. But it's such a remote possibility. Don't worry about it my dear.

EUGENIA (*suddenly sharp*). Nikolai, we both know what they're going to do. (*Loud.*) Let's not pretend, all right. (*Pause. She looks across at him. Loud*:) Why didn't you tell me ever?

NIKOLAI. Tell you what?

EUGENIA. Tell me what you were doing — what your work was. I heard it from Polya — all these ideas. (*Looking at him.*) Didn't I have a right to know?

NIKOLAI. I did not discuss such things with you . . . you knew that.

EUGENIA (*her head going back, quiet*). Yes, I knew that.

They're sitting wide apart in the carriage, SASHA *crouching in the corner, the phones ringing in the distance.*

I don't know how long we've got — when they're going to come back, maybe in the middle. (*Tracing a pattern on the wall with her finger, not looking at him.*) I have no idea if I can go through with this . . . but if I don't say it now I'm never going to be able to say it. (*Tension is in her voice. She is trying to keep control.*)

NIKOLAI. Eugenia, what is it?

EUGENIA (*with real force suddenly*). I want you to realise what it was like, Nikolai, before, our lives together. Before we came here. (*Forcing herself to say it.*) What it meant for me . . . how . . . how (*Forcing herself.*) how I had to support and not ask, (*Not looking at him.*) give to you but never touch, serve (*Quieter.*) but never . . .

NIKOLAI (*cutting her off*). I don't know you should say these things now — the boy is here, Sasha is here.

EUGENIA. I have to, Kolia — I have to tell you. (*Quiet with feeling.*) But it isn't easy. (*Not looking at him.*) Your work — this enormous weight in the air always, a world I was forbidden to enter . . . but for some reason I always believed in it, I don't doubt it for a moment, I know it's real.

But my God, when you left me in the country how I hated those summers, those horrible summers, endless languid days and how I *hated* you sometimes. (*A momentary look at him.*) Yes.

NIKOLAI (*looking up*). Hated me? Eugenia . . .

EUGENIA (*with feeling*). I could hardly think for myself. Waiting for you . . . all the time waiting for you to *see* me, to discuss with me, *anything*, to *acknowledge* me.

If I ever have to live through that again with me festering underneath, (*Matter of fact.*) beginning to scream and cry inside . . . (*Holding herself.*) I felt there was so much in here . . . trapped in here . . . it was like burrowing out of a grave.

Nikolai, forgive me. (*Pause.*) But . . . (*She stops.*)

NIKOLAI. Go on, proceed. Say what you have to say.

EUGENIA (*who has looked up, is staring at him*). This is the most difficult conversation of my life — if I look at you I can't go on.

Trying to keep control — after waivering, her voice incisive again.

But if I don't try to do it I won't be able to cope afterwards at all.

She turns away, leaning against the side, forcing herself to go on.

It's just the daring it took to break with all I'd thought before — and do the few things I did, forging documents, making up train times, tiny little acts which led to my getting that job, . . . absurd as it may seem now they were terribly important at the time, the release I felt doing that, it was extraordinarily strong — what welled up because of that . . .

She looks up again.

What I am trying to tell you is, though you seem to have been completely oblivious of it over these last months. (*Pause.*) But it changed my life, Nikolai, I want you to understand that, (*Pause.*) because otherwise . . . if you go away now . . . I feel there're things we never said . . . and then . . .

She stops.

Oh, Nikolai, say something, help me —

Silence.

NIKOLAI (*detached tone*). It is very interesting I think . . .

EUGENIA. What is — is that all you can say? (*Sharp*:) At this
time . . .

NIKOLAI (*continuing, not looking at her*). Large events, great
events even, have happened just outside, and we've seen most
of them — or heard most of them to be more accurate.
Meanwhile in here, locked up in this, squashed into this
matchbox.

EUGENIA. Rather a large matchbox, Nikolai.

NIKOLAI (*continuing, detached tone*). And yet the energy
generated in here, felt at times, if you will allow the slight
exaggeration, felt it could flatten city walls. It seems to me,
Eugenia, in this messy clump of all of us, all of us tangled up
together, a way was found of releasing our separate energies.
(*Pause.*) Unlocking things.

EUGENIA (*not looking at him, sharp*). That's how you'd put it is
it?

NIKOLAI (*slowly*). And I know some of that (*Staring at her.*) . . .
a lot of that is because of you.

Silence, EUGENIA *looks up.*

EUGENIA. Yes it is. (*She looks at him.*) And Polya . . .

NIKOLAI (*staring at her*). Just because I find certain things
difficult to say doesn't mean they aren't true. (*Slight pause.*)
I've been meaning to say many things to you.

EUGENIA. Yes.

NIKOLAI (*slight smile*). And you know before this I never could
think on trains — I never had an idea on one in my life.

EUGENIA (*looking at him, but not yet moving to him*). Kolia, is
there anything we can do when they come?

NIKOLAI. No — (*Detached tone:*) it is interesting when I think
usually, I nearly always have some sense of the future; you can
see distant shapes, people you are about to meet, ideas you are
about to have. For some weeks there's been nothing there, just
a rather dark cold void.

SASHA. I know, Papa.

The light has imperceptibly changed, the place oppressive.

EUGENIA. Yes — it suddenly seems to be growing smaller in here.

NIKOLAI. It appears to be shrinking because we're locked in.

EUGENIA. It's claustrophobic for the first time. Suddenly it's rather horrible.

SASHA (*moving over to his father*). Papa, I'm sorry, I am, I am so sorry, Papa.

NIKOLAI (*detached tone*). Yes, but there's no need for that. You know I never thought waiting for one's possible execution one's mind would be so clear. It's a pleasant surprise. It's *interesting* to find that . . .

EUGENIA (*suddenly moving over to him, touching him*). Kolia, don't say that any more, stop that. Look at me. You don't have to talk like that. (*Touching him.*) I can't believe I may have to say goodbye to you. (*Looking at him.*) I'm deliberately refusing to try.

The door bangs open. GUARDS 1 *and* 2 *enter.*

NIKOLAI (*calmly*). So here you are, you left rather suddenly. I didn't know whether you were coming back.

GUARD 1. Nikolai Pesiakoff, you are under arrest — you have to come with us now. You may bring no personal belongings.

GUARD 2. Don't cause us trouble, you've had time to say goodbye by now.

NIKOLAI. What is the charge?

GUARD 1. You know perfectly well — apart from trying to remove valuables unlawfully from this country, you have lied about being a government official; both are capital offences.

GUARD 2. The Minister of Labour you referred to, they'd never heard of him when we telephoned. We told them to look again, they think he's been arrested.

GUARD 1 (*pulling and tearing apart what remains of* NIKOLAI's *equipment*). These ridiculous scraps shouldn't be here.

The two GUARDS *hurl the pieces out of the carriage. They move, bulky dangerous presences around the carriage, bludgeoning the place apart, getting rid of things.*

(*To* NIKOLAI). Right, stand up — time to move.

EUGENIA (*staring up*). You going to try to take him just like that are you? No shoes.

GUARD 2. That's how we have to do it.

EUGENIA (*suddenly*). How dare you treat somebody like that — how dare you touch him.

GUARD 1. Don't try to get yourself arrested as well — it is not something I want to have to do.

EUGENIA. And how dare you not believe me. (*Staring at them.*) Didn't you hear him tell you what he did — he worked for the Northern Railway.

SASHA. He did!

GUARD 1. He could never have.

EUGENIA (*cutting him off*). We wouldn't make up such a mad lie.

GUARD 1. Many do.

EUGENIA. How do you *know* he's not? I'll prove it to you. (*Sharp, keeping her eyes on them.*) Do you know who the station master is for instance at Vologda, come on who is he? Tell me. Sergei Goncharov — (*Before they can stop her:*) — or do you know for instance what is now different about the night train from Omsk to Moscow, have either of you any idea?

GUARD 1 (*watching her, intrigued*). No.

EUGENIA. Of course you don't — it is the first time a through Express has ever been run on that line, it's being run for an experimental period of three months.

GUARD 1 (*intrigued smile*). An uncommon sight — a woman spouting railway statistics from the heart!

EUGENIA. Don't you patronise me, Comrade — (*Staring at him.*)

When is the delivery expected of the new locomotives, the ones built entirely in this country? October 31st.

GUARD 2 (*disbelieving*). Really?

EUGENIA. How many suburban lines are about to open in Moscow. Four, with a total of forty-two stations, the original plan was for fifty, go and check that one, go on, you will find it is totally accurate. And while we're about it, when is the new phone exchange having its official opening, the one that will serve a third of the city? Only a very few people know the official date, do you think you could find anybody at this border that knows that — it is September 14th. (*Watching them.*) Tell me how could we possibly know these things — unless *he* was the telephone examiner of the Northern District. (*Loud:*) What other conceivable explanation is there, just let me hear you suggest another?

Startled pause.

(*Very forceful:*) You have no legal right to arrest this man and if what I tell you is true, which it is, you could be making a grave mistake, Comrade, for which you will be responsible. Don't you try to touch him again — I warn you, don't you maltreat him again in any way. (*Loud:*) Go on, let go of him, and let us be on our way at once.

EUGENIA *faces them, the phone ringing in the background.*

GUARD 1 (*staring at her*). Madame . . .

GUARD 2 (*tense*). We've got another load to deal with in three minutes, it's coming in now.

GUARD 1 (*staring at her*). I am making this decision for the wrong reasons and I will regret it, because none of the evidence adds up, these scraps of metals — (*Flings the last one through the door.*) the look of the place. But for one moment, a moment that will no doubt seem absurd tomorrow, (*Staring at EUGENIA.*) you have convinced me, Comrade, that he did indeed do that job. I have no idea why — look at the man! (*Pointing at NIKOLAI sitting in the middle of the carriage.*) But you have. There still remains the diamonds. We will say we found them on another train. I will make no record of this incident. Nor of your departure, none will exist anywhere.

They both move.

I don't advise you *ever* to try to come back.

They both leave. Silence.

NIKOLAI (*calmly*). You truly can be said, without exaggeration, to be the Telephone Examiner of the Northern District.

EUGENIA (*leaning her head against the side*). Not for long, not in a few minutes . . .

An ear-splitting screech, the sound of a locomotive backs up towards them, a piercing sound of movement and violent braking that touches the pit of the stomach.

EUGENIA. Oh God. (*Turning her head.*) I really don't want to go — how much you realise it now, when you can't turn back. (*Very quiet.*) I wish something would happen to stop us going.

NIKOLAI. Yes. I will have lost the race too, Eugenia, to be the first in my work, I have no money or resources now.

EUGENIA. You did it, though. I know you did. We know we existed.

The crunch of a locomotive up close, the sounds are very violent, wrenching.

NIKOLAI (*slight smile*). Yes, I can see myself bleating out in an omnibus in the middle of London, a hunched figure on the back seat, pointing at a queue outside a talking motion picture house and saying I was the first to do that! — and we started from much further behind.

SASHA (*moving*). I will write it up here, Papa, I will leave it on the wall, a record, there must be a record, the date . . . and what happened here.

The carriage begins to shake.

EUGENIA (*quiet*). I wonder what this is going to be used for, what's going to be put in here.

NIKOLAI (*his tone loud and angry*). BUT WHAT WE COULD HAVE DONE EUGENIA IF WE'D STAYED . . .

EUGENIA (*lying down as the carriage shakes, slowly curling up, trying to control the emotions*). I know — I know that.

NIKOLAI (*really loud*). There was a great deal more to be done. (*Pause. The loud, tearing noise of the train as it moves.*) And God knows what's on the track. What already has been disposed of — we're crunching over, passing over it as we move.

Loud, violent noise.

EUGENIA (*looking around the carriage*). People going to be herded in here by the hundred.

SASHA (*trying to write with a knife on the woodwork*). I can't make it write . . . (*Loud:*) Oh god, I can't make it write.

NIKOLAI (*quietly*). I'm just beginning to experience that tearing at the insides, Eugenia, that feeling cutting through one . . . of helplessness. It's much colder suddenly, Eugenia.

EUGENIA (*curled up, letting out a cry of anger*). I don't want to leave.

NIKOLAI. No, my love.

The lights fade fast so they disappear into darkness as the carriage lights go out; the loud noise of movement continues.

My God, it's cold. This is the worse part, can you still see me, can you? (*Louder:*) Can you?

EUGENIA. Just. (EUGENIA *curls up as the carriage shakes.*) Just . . . I don't want to go, Nikolai. I . . . (*Loud:*) I don't . . . I don't want to leave.